Adhd

Parenting

Learn How to Heal Child Suffering From Adhd

(A Learning Guide for Women and Teens to Gain Motivation)

Lyle Gray

Published by Rob Miles

© **Lyle Gray**

All Rights Reserved

Adhd Parenting: Learn How to Heal Child Suffering From Adhd (A Learning Guide for Women and Teens to Gain Motivation)

ISBN 978-1-990084-19-5

Legal & Disclaimer

Table of Contents

Introduction

The role of the parent is probably one of the most precarious careers in the world. The responsibility of molding the minds of young ones, shaping them into responsible adults, and motivating them to be all they can be can be a daunting one. Even under the best of circumstances, parents are fraught with worry about the right thing to do.

These things weigh heavy on a parent's mind and rightly so. It is perfectly natural to want your child to succeed and take their place in the world. No matter where you come from, what culture fosters you, or even what genetic background forms you, the parents play the most important part of your child's life as their primary guidance counselors.

So, it stands to reason that when a child begins to struggle or loses interest in life in general, is distracted or can't control his emotions it would be a legitimate and necessary cause of concern. The fact that you are reading this book is proof that you are like most other parents in search of answers to the hard questions.

Watching a child who has to fight every day just to perform the most basic of functions that his peers can do easily is hard. It often forces parents to seek for answers in areas outside of their field of expertise and in light of a lack of understanding of the issues affecting their child. Sadly, they often tend to look for these answers in all the wrong places. They listen to the well-intentioned advice of their friends and family, they trust the words of the counselors and teachers at school, and they search blogs, forums, and all manner of websites on the Internet.

While it is with good intentions that these myriads of people try to steer them to their way of thinking, the solutions they offer are often not what your child needs. You've probably already heard many of them and may have even tried some of their suggestions to no avail.

It's just a matter of getting tough with your child

Medication is the answer

The problem is with the school

You're coddling them

Give them rewards

Don't give them rewards

They're just testing you

Chances are, you've tried all of these suggestions, listened to every comment and even tried negotiating and pleading with your child and received little to no positive results in return. Adding to your turmoil, there will inevitably come conflicts at home, and you're dealing with what seems to be an ever growing struggle over household chores, homework, and power struggles with siblings.

Now, you're wondering what is wrong with your child. Perhaps you have heard of ADHD from a teacher or relative who has observed something in your child. Whatever the case, the best solution to the situation is to find out what it is and whether this is what's driving your child's erratic behavior. It is said that "Ignorance is bliss," but that is only true when there is no risk of loss. A parent knows that her best defense is knowledge. The more informed you are about your child, the better equipped you'll be to deal with the issue.

In this regard, you, the parent, are the only one that can shed light on the topic. You may consult with your family physician, talk with school counselors and teachers, even glean valuable information on the Internet but always keep these individuals in their proper place. You know your child, you are the one who knows their weaknesses, strengths, desires, tendencies and the intimate nature of their personalities. None of these advisors – no matter how much knowledge they have – can tell you your child has ADHD without your personal input.

Through the pages of this book, we will help you cut through all of the confusion and give you a clear cut vision of what ADHD really is. We'll point out the tell-tale signs that can help you to analyze your child's own behavior and guide your focus in a direction that will best benefit your child.

In part one, we'll break down and explain why children with ADHD are different and what it means for them. How you can determine your child's own weaknesses and strengths and how your actions actually do have an impact on your children and what they do.

In part two, we'll give you the tools you need to work with your child giving him direction and a plan of action that can and in most cases will lead to success. Like George Peppard used to say, "I love it when a plan comes together," when you have a plan to tackle ADHD head on, then you'll love the affect it will have on your child and by extension your entire family. The reality is simple. The sooner you can pinpoint ADHD in your child and develop a workable course of action the sooner your child can began to share some of those same experiences all children have.

Childhood is a precious time in all of our lives, but if your child is truly struggling with ADHD, then he is likely missing out on many of those golden opportunities. Opportunities that make and shape the person he is meant to be, the building blocks of adulthood. There is no time like the present to give him the tools to master these challenges and ensure that your child benefits from those golden moments that will last him the rest of his life.

There are plenty of books on this subject on the market, thanks again for choosing this one! Every effort was made to ensure it is full of as much useful information as possible, please enjoy!

Chapter 1: Adhd – Attention Deficit Hyperactivity Disorder

Is a condition known for well over 50 years, and it's shaped around three major symptoms: difficulty sustaining attention, hyperactivity and impulsive behavior. There is no known cause for why this happens, but there are lots of theories ranging from genetics, social and environmental factors to nutrition. Scientific research about this condition has shown that, in people with this disorder, certain brain areas are irrigated with blood differently; some small parts of the prefrontal cortex receive a higher amount of blood. Further studies have found that neurotransmitters may have a relation with the disorder, and the main one, to be at fault, was found to be Dopamine, with some involvement of Norepinephrine. If neurotransmitters don't work the way they are supposed to, there are different conditions that can emerge, one of these conditions is ADHD.

In recent years this condition has become the most commonly diagnosed behavioral disorder of childhood. The other problem this brings us too is that ADHD doesn't only affect youngsters; it remains with a person and reflects in their adult life. Even if adults have the power to hide it from others, and to motivate themselves, they too, feel the full power of the symptoms, being a better actor only helps them integrate better. Only the perspective changes, the challenges remain the same.

Despite the fact that ADHD is not a life threatening condition, it affects children's ability to learn, and they perform poorly in school because they lack the patience to stay still and focus on a single task at once. Eventually, they will begin to lack self-confidence and will become frustrated. Frustration leads to irritability and, sometimes, aggressive behavior, which in turn leads to being rejected by the group, resulting in more frustration. It's a closed circle that must be broken in order to develop properly.

Most children show noticeable signs of ADHD early on in life, some as early as 3 years of age, but it's usually diagnosed at ages between 6 and 12, when the child is in school. Commonly, in these cases, the teachers are the ones to signal the problem.

The most common symptoms a child will show are: Frequent daydreaming, difficulty following through on instructions, apparently not listening, problems organizing tasks or activities, easily distracted, fidgeting or squirming, excessively talkative, difficulty remaining seated and seemingly in constant motion.

Many children exhibit these symptoms, but not all of them suffer from this condition. It is difficult to diagnose and it often happens to be misdiagnosed. Over the past years the media attention, that ADHD received, has led to an increase in children found to suffer from it. Although many children could have been wrongly diagnosed, there is insufficient data to support such a statement. Nevertheless, the fact remains that there is no specific test to confirm the diagnosis.

One of the challenges children with ADHD face is being blamed for their behavior although they shouldn't be. People shouldn't consider their behavior as a choice; in order to improve they need the right kind of help.

It is important to know, that most healthy children tend to be hyperactive, and it is common knowledge that children are not attentive to things or actions that they don't like.

Also, one of the major challenges in discovering this condition is the fact that gifted children exhibit, what it is known ADHD symptoms.

Gifted children who are bored will daydream, and not take part in tasks that seem irrelevant. They will not complete projects that become boring in time. They will question rules, customs and traditions and this can lead to power struggles with authorities. They are active by nature and need less sleep.

A child may be gifted and also suffer from ADHD but, in most cases he just needs extra attention and more activities that are interesting to him. Even if such a child doesn't fit in the pattern that society has imposed, with proper care and the right amount of exercise and nutrients he will fit in and excel in most things.

Modern medicine encourages, or should I say, overly encourages, the use of medication in order to control symptoms. Some of these drugs are able to reduce hyperactivity and impulsive behavior, others help them obtain better focus but, they do come with side effects.

There are two types of medication commonly used: Stimulants and Non-stimulants.

Stimulants are made from amphetamine and methylphenidate. They prescribe these drugs to children, due to the medical advantages that they bring. They stimulate parts of the brain and help focus on time consuming tasks. This is one of the reasons for witch stimulants are sold on the black market, students and business men use them to help with learning for exams or for developing difficult projects.

You are probably wandering how could a stimulant help calm down a child who is already over stimulated. The answer is simple. The drug stimulates a precise part of the brain which helps balance energy, in favor of concentration and enhanced focus.

Although this sounds great, especially if your child has problems in school, parents must be aware of the consequences. There is little research about what happens in the long run. Studies were mainly focused on the immediate effects, and these drugs work very fast, sometimes in a matter of hours. The side effects of using stimulants range from loss of appetite that can cause weight loss and sometimes a slow growth rate, insomnia to developing tics. There were some reports of people dying from taking stimulants, but extremely rare.

It is important to remember that stimulants are exactly what it's written on the label: drugs, and you can never let your child self-medicate, not even if he is an adolescent. Abusing stimulants can have severe consequences.

Non-stimulant Medication is relatively new, and was introduced to address those who didn't tolerate stimulants well. It works differently, by increasing the activity of Norepinephrine in the brain. They are similar to antidepressants, and take longer to work, results are seen only in a few weeks, sometimes even months. Side effects are different too; they make children somewhat lethargic and cause nausea.

Even if medication sounds appealing from time to time, it only manages the effects of ADHD; it does nothing to cure it. The ugly truth is that many parents that have placed their children on medication didn't just notice an improvement in behavior; they saw their own child's personality change under their eyes. This is not a pretty picture, we all want what is best for our children but sometimes the right choice is not the simplest.

Thankfully, the medical world didn't just give us drugs; it also gave us people able to think outside of the box, for a change. And these amazing people developed natural, healthy, side effects free, ways to help our children overcome the difficulties that ADHD presents. Ways like the nutritional and the behavioral approach.

Chapter 2: Children With Adhd Have Trouble With:

Inattention, hyperactivity, and impulsivity which are the key behaviors of ADHD. It is normal for all children to be inattentive, hyperactive, or impulsive sometimes, but for children with ADHD, these behaviors are more severe and occur more often. To be diagnosed with the disorder, a child must have symptoms for 6 or more months, starts before age 7 and to a degree that is greater than other children of the same age.

Symptoms of inattention

Paying attention, these children are easily distracted, forget things, forget details and often switch from one activity to another without completing any.

Controlling impulsive behaviors (may act without thinking about what the result will be), and in some cases, are overly active.

Have difficulty focusing

Difficulty with organizing

Unless they are doing something they enjoy they become bored very easily. They do not seem to listen when spoken to.

Daydream and become confused easily.

Very forgetful, struggle to follow instructions.

Trouble completing homework and turning it in.

Always losing things (e.g., pencils, books, toys assignments.)

Children who have symptoms of hyperactivity may:

Fidget and squirm in their seats

Talk nonstop

Dash around, touching or playing with anything and everything in sight

Have trouble sitting still during dinner, school, and story time

Be constantly in motion

Have difficulty doing quiet tasks or activities.

Children who have symptoms of impulsivity may:

Be very impatient.

Blurt out inappropriate comments, show their emotions without restraint, and act without regard for consequences

Have difficulty waiting for things they want or waiting their turns in games.

Often interrupt conversations or others' activities.

These children are often picky eaters only eating 2 or 3 types of food, and have trouble sleeping.

What Causes ADHD?

Genes may play a large role in someone being diagnosed with ADHD although there are several other factors that may play a large part. As with many other disabilities, there is no one explanation that can be given for why a child or adult has a learning disability. Many factors may be responsible for learning disabilities.

Some researchers believe that learning disabilities result from complications that occur before, during, or shortly after birth. Males are more likely to have a learning disability than females. Learning disabilities tend to occur in families. So if a parent has ADHD it is likely that one or more of their children will have ADHD.

According to the National Institute of Mental Health

Scientists are not sure what causes ADHD, although many studies suggest that genes play a large role. Like so many other illnesses, ADHD probably results from a number of factors including genetics. Researchers are also looking at environmental factors, and are studying how brain injuries, nutrition, and the social environment might contribute to ADHD.

Genes. Genes are the blueprint we inherit from our parents. Studies show that ADHD often runs in families. Researchers are looking at several genes that may make people more likely to develop the disorder.

Environmental factors. Studies suggest there may be a link between cigarette smoking and alcohol use during pregnancy and ADHD in children. Scientists are studying the use of alcohol during pregnancy. Children also inhale whatever is in the environment or in the air and it get into the lungs of these children.

Chemicals

Chemicals are also found in the carpets in your homes, upholstery, rugs, mattresses, soaps and toothpaste and the list goes on. Chemicals are also found on the clothes that you dry clean.

Additives, Coloring and Dyes

Many people believe that additives, coloring and dyes contribute to hyperactivity and inattention.

There have been a lot of studies on the effects of artificial food dyes on children, dating back to the 1970s. Some showed that food dyes could cause behavioral problems in children, and others didn't.

Studies suggest that when certain dyes and coloring are removed from the diet the symptoms were reduced.

Preservatives

Some parents and caregivers believe that preservatives have a negative effect on some children's behavior which can affect their ability to learn. You may want to cut out preservatives from your child diet for a period of time and monitor if there was a negative effect or not.

The issue is controversial with experts offering at times opposing views at times.

Food Sensitivities

A large number of children who have been diagnosed with ADHD may be sensitive to eating certain foods, which may be the primary cause of their ADHD. This response may be the primary cause of their ADHD. In what type of child should you suspect food allergies?

Here is a list of some symptoms that may result from food sensitivities in certain children:

Hyperactivity

Changes in mood

Halitosis

Sleep disturbances

Delay in sleep onset

Migraines

Other headaches

Abdominal pain

Bedwetting

Tantrums

Eczema

Asthma

Seizures

Research shows that by treating the food allergies all of these symptoms can be relieved.

If you see your child's symptoms in this list it is possible that food allergies may be contributing to his problem. If your child has allergies such as asthma then food allergies most certainly will be contributing to their problem.

You may want to have your child tested for food allergies or you can play detective and try to figure out what your child is allergic to by eliminating a certain food for a period of about two weeks and observe them.

Gluten Free Diet

In a small study, children with ADHD had been put on a Gluten free diet, foods that are free of gluten such as acorn, amaranth, garbanzo, beans, brown rice and buckwheat. Behavior changes had improved and the children had an increased attention span and were able to focus better.

Sulfites are sulfur-based compounds that may be added to foods as an enhancer and preservative. Sulfites can also be found in cooked and processed foods. Always read food labels to check for sulfites.

Some sulfite-containing ingredients to look for on food labels include:

Sulfur dioxide

Potassium bisulfite or potassium metabisulfite

Sodium bisulfite, sodium metabisulfite, or sodium sulfite

Some foods that contain sulfites include:

Baked goods

Pickled foods

Dried fruits

Canned vegetables

Trail mix

Teas

Soup mixes

Be sure to read labels.

Mono Sodium Glutamate (MSG)

Monosodium glutamate enhances the flavor of food and is add to foods like canned vegetables, so I would avoid canned foods, processed meats such as hot dogs and cold cuts, Chinese food, soy sauce and other foods.

MSG is also contained in additives that say:

Calciun caseinate

Sodiun caseinate

Autolyzed yeast

Anything hydrolyzed

When eating at restaurants ask if their foods contain MSG if it does contain MSG ask if they can leave it out of your food.

Pesticides

Pesticides are a common concern especially outside the home and on the food that our children eat. Pesticides are toxic and our children eat it, our food is sprayed with it, and it is also used to kill bugs and insects and spray the lawns. Children eat these foods and play on the lawn which they then absorb these toxins.

Preschoolers are exposed to high levels of lead which are found in old plumbing fixtures or paint in old buildings. These children have a higher risk of developing

ADHD because small children tend to bite on the edges of and swallow the paint.

Sugar. A lot of people got the idea that using refined sugar makes the ADHD child hyper-activity worse. Research does not support this.

Food additives. Recent British research indicates a possible link between consumption of certain food additives like artificial colors or preservatives. Research is under way to confirm the findings and to learn more about how food additives may affect hyperactivity.

Scientist is also studying the use of alcohol and tobacco during pregnancy.

Chapter 3: Risk Factors Of Adhd

There are many factors responsible for the cause of this medical condition, they are as follows:
Injuries of the brain
Size of the child at birth
Environmental exposure to toxins such as lead
Exposure to certain toxins during pregnancy
Medication during pregnancy
Alcohol intake
Smoking could be a cause Gene
NOTE: This medical condition is more predominant in male child than the female; females with this condition usually have the following problems:
They lack attention
Anxiety
They are usually depressed
They have learning disabilities
They are usually addicted
TREATMENTS AND THERAPIES

Researchers say there are no cure for this medical condition, but in the other hand lifestyle changes and combination medication can serve as help to ADHD.
The notable approach to treating ADHD could help in the reduction of its symptoms and also facilitate functioning, they are:
Medication
Psychotherapy
Training processes
Educational processes
Combining treatment could also be of help
For MEDICATION, stimulants will help to stimulate the regulatory center. This stimulant helps to increase the normal brain function. This chemical substance is called dopamine which has a role to play in attention and thinking.
Some health condition such as:
Heart disease
Seizure

Hypertension

Kidney disease

Liver disease

Glaucoma

Will need an instruction from the doctor before an intake of any stimulant, and if in the process of taking any stimulants, the above diseased condition surfaces, or talk to your doctor if you see any of the following under-listed side effects:

Loss of appetite

Lack of sleep

Tics

Fatigue

Personal changes

Stomach ache

Irritability

PSYCHOTHERAPY AND SOCIAL INTERVENTION

Some social functions have really shown improvement in patient and it does help then to improve day to day activities. Also those with this medical

condition   needs
Attention
Guidance
Understanding
From their parents and siblings for proper
functioning   of
their   child.
BEHAVIORAL THERAPY

This process really helps the patient to
change his or her behavior. This therapy
really involves the use of some
practical aspects such as:
Doing   school   works
Solving   emotional   problems
This aspect relates and teaches on:
How to be mindful of one's behavior
To be sensitive to things Thought

Chapter 4: Stay Healthy And Think Positive

Parents of ADHD sufferers should set a platform for the children's physical and emotional health. A parent has full control over certain factors that can influence the symptoms of the child's condition.

Positive Attitude Yields Positive Results

You need to demonstrate positivity at all times if you really want to succeed in your endeavor. If you will exude a positive attitude and common sense at all times, then you will be able to bring great help to your child with ADHD. If you are calm and focused, then there is a huge possibility to impart such feeling and attitude to your child, and help him stay focused and calm, as well.

Never let your thoughts go astray and always keep in mind that your child's behavior is due to the condition that he or she suffers from, and most of the time those actions are unintentional. Keeping a good sense of humor is helpful during such times. What might be seen as an embarrassing situation today can turn into a funny and a heartwarming family story in the near future. Keep those in your treasure chest of memories, and find delight in cherishing the fruit of your struggles when you finally see your child doing things that he should be accomplishing all by himself.

Learn to compromise, and avoid worrying too much about the things that are happening right now. Avoid regarding an unfinished chore/task as your failure, especially if your child was able to complete three other tasks for the day.

You should not set your standards too high, and avoid being a perfectionist. If you do that, then your child with ADHD will always fall short of your expectations, and that will only lead to frustrations that he will surely feel. Instead of helping your child, making him feel your frustrations will only cause further destruction to his life and your entire family.

Believe that your child can do things on his own with little or no supervision from you, if you just give him enough time. Think about all the positive, unique, and worthy attributes of your child, and write them all down. Put your faith on him, and believe that he will be able to mature, change, learn, and finally succeed in life. Keep these positive things about your child, and the things that he will be able to do in the future, with your consistent guidance. Recite them in your head like a mantra while doing your daily chores.

Live a Healthy Life and Keep your Positivity for as Long as it takes

You are your children's source of strength, so you should always keep your body healthy and fit. Take time to rest to avoid getting excessively tired that might trigger you to lose your patience and composure, and might in turn cause you to blame everything to your children, especially the one with ADHD.

If you need to take care of your children, then you also need to take care of yourself. Set the right meal for you, and make sure it will give you strength and vigor to carry out the task at hand with success. Exercise for a fit body and find ways to lessen your stress (you could meditate in the morning and enjoy a luxurious aromatic bath at night). If you get sick, then consult a doctor right away.

You and your spouse should be each other's pillar during the challenging times of your lives. You can also seek support from your own siblings, parents, relatives, and friends. The point is you don't have to go through it all alone. You can also talk to your child's doctors, teachers, and therapist. Find something that will keep you holding on especially during those times when giving up seems to be the most promising thing to do.

If someone in your family offers to take care of your child with ADHD, then don't hesitate to grab the opportunity although you might feel a bit guilty. Tell them honestly the things they need to know about your child's behavior, and the best way to address the problem in case he has tantrums. Giving them enough knowledge about your child can make you feel less guilty, and enjoy your little time off and relax.

Chapter 5: The Medical Cure

Traditional Treatment

Prescribed medication is often used to eliminate or decrease the symptoms of ADHD, but there is little evidence to endorse its efficiency.

As the disorder has become more widely recognized, more drugs have been introduced onto the market to deal with it. In some cases, there is no doubt that medicine can be helpful but in others, it has been found to produce unpleasant and risky side effects. At its best, medication can help ease some of the symptoms while others remain and, of course, if medication stops, then so does any relief, which may have been found.

The fact that drugs, which treat ADHD, can trigger harmful side effects may suggest that traditional medicine is not always the best solution. There are two types of drug treatment: stimulant and non-stimulant. They act by affecting the amount of dopamine produced by the brain. Dopamine is a neurotransmitter, which stimulates the brain to action, or motivation and can help some sufferers to concentrate more whilst reducing their hyperactivity. Drugs under this category include Ritalin, Dexedrine and Adderall. While drugs are an effective answer for many, others can be badly affected by their use. The side effects of stimulants, which may become apparent are:

- Difficulty sleeping

- Loss of appetite or stomach upsets

- Palpitations

- Dizziness

- Tics

- Depression

- Bad temper

- Irritability

- Headaches

- Restlessness

Even if these side effects were to be discounted, there is still uncertainty about the long-term physical and mental impact. ADHD is a fairly recent phenomenon and drugs, which may be used to treat it, can exacerbate other problems present within the body.

Research so far has been insufficient to be able to discount detrimental effects on brain development. Stimulants are open to being abused and teenagers can and do use them to give them an unnatural boost. They might also be responsible for precipitating psychiatric problems because they are altering the chemical compounds of the brain. Stimulants have also been found to be the cause of cardiac arrest in those with a pre-existing heart condition.

If the person is taking the stimulant medication experiences any of the following symptoms you should contact your doctor immediately:

- Paranoia
- Chest pains
- Hallucinating
- Shortness of breath

- Fainting

The non-stimulant drug, Strattera, does not fare much better although does have fewer side-effects. It does not affect the dopamine in the brain but instead influences another chemical in the brain called norepinephrine. It also acts as an anti-depressant but is found to be not as effective as stimulants. It can also still produce side effects, which include:

- Nausea

- Headaches

- Vomiting

- Pain in the abdomen

- Sleepiness

- Moodiness

- Dizziness

It is small wonder that interest in natural remedies has been piqued in an effort to avoid unpleasant and, in some cases, dangerous side-effects. It could even be proven that damage done to the brain by these drugs offers disproportionately low respite and reward.

In the next chapter, we will explore how drugs can be abandoned and replaced by natural remedies. What can you incorporate into a lifestyle, sometimes very easily, to eradicate the symptoms of ADHD or at least improve them as much as the traditional medication promises?

Chapter 6: Identifying And Treating Adult Adhd

In the past, ADHD waт mainly considered an academic or school iттue for children. ADHD, however, iт a 24 hour a day condition.

It not only impairт тchool or work functioning, it also can have a тignificant impact on familieт and тocial relationтhipт. There is even a high incidence of divorce in families in which a member haт ADHD.

When a child iт firтt diagnoтed with ADHD, it is important to

alтo тcreen the reтt of the family to determine whether additional family memberт have ADHD. Once family memberт

with ADHD are diagnoтed, treatment can begin -- and other family members can begin to make тenтe of the challengeт

they've been encountering. By properly identifying ADHD in individualт, treatment can be тo much more effective and family life much more joyful.

Treating ADHD

ADHD is typically treated from a number of angleт. Medicationт, тuch aт ritalin, are uтed to increase attention. Behavioral therapy interventionт are uтed to condition behaviorт

conducive to better relationships, learning opportunitieт, and diтcipline. And mindfulneтт is taught to help sufferers of ADHD

learn to concentrate for extended periods of time.

21 Traditional treatment of ADHD iт far from perfect. Ritalin can come with тignificant тide effectт, and behavioral interventions are hard to implement outside the therapiтt'т room. For thiт

reaтon, reтearcherт are still looking for alternatives, and CBD

has come under the microтcope

Medications used for ADHD

Two typeτ of drugτ are approved to treat ADHD: τtimulantτ and non-τtimulantτ.

☐ Stimulants. Stimulant drugτ are the moτt commonly

uτed medicationτ to treat ADHD. Stimulantτ work by

increaτing brain chemicalτ, including dopamine, that are

critical for tranτmitting meττageτ between brain neurons. In kidτ, 70 to 80 percent τhow improvement in τymptomτ within one to two hourτ of taking the

medication. In adults, 70 percent report noticeable

improvement from τtimulantτ within hourτ of uτing the medication.

The two generic τtimulantτ, alτo known aτ central nervouτ τyτtem stimulants, that are widely uτed to treat ADHD are methylphenidate (Concerta, Aptenτio XR) and dextro-amphetamine (Adderall).

☐ **Nonstimulants.** In cases where a stimulant drug is not well tolerated or preferred, there is atomoexetine

(Straterra), a non-stimulant that helps increase a brain chemical called norepinephrine. This chemical can help

improve focus, while tamping down impulsiveness and hyperactivity. Clonidine (Kapvay) and Guanfacine 22

(Intuniv) are also non-stimulants and work slightly differently to achieve similar effects.

Therapy

Cognitive behavioral therapy and psychoeducation are

recommended for people with ADHD to provide a framework for how to better manage emotions and general behavior.

Therapy can also focus on strategies to help with self- regulation and self-monitoring. This education can help a child or adult with ADHD as they face day-to-day challenge's at home, in the classroom, at work, and in social situations. In addition, social skills groups can be beneficial for children and teens with ADHD, who often struggle with their social interactions, due to impulsivity. Therapy usually occurs one time per week, for 45

minutes at a time.

A therapist may also recommend alternative therapies and/or dietary changes that have proven helpful with managing different symptoms of ADHD. These may include:

☐ Meditation and mindfulness exercises to address the

anxiety so often associated with ADHD.

☐ Working with an ADHD coach to learn organizational techniques and other day-to-day coping skills.

☐ Emotional freedom technique (EFT). Also known as

tapping, EFT involves using the fingers to tap on a series of meridians on the body that can activate emotional releaᴛe and healing.

23 ☐ neurofeedback training (or EEG biofeedback) is utilized in an attempt to teach/train one who struggles with ADHD to produce the brain wave patternᴛ aᴛᴛociated with focuᴛ.

☐ Dietary improvementᴛ that focus on eating foodᴛ that reduce inflammation in the body, which in turn can help the brain function more optimally. Thiᴛ includes limiting white flour, white sugar, proceᴛᴛed foods, and incorporating more fruitᴛ and vegetables, aᴛ well aᴛ

omega-3 fatty acid rich foods such aᴛ walnutᴛ and ᴛalmon.

Chapter 7: Adhd: How It May Manifest In Your Child

ADHD can take several forms in children. It is not difficult to track the child with ADHD who is very chaotic. Boys generally come into this category. But then there are some types of ADHD which go undiagnosed because their effects in children are less outwardly evident. This happens mainly in case of girls.

ADHD in children has several indications such as lack of concentration power, impulsive behavior and inability to sit still for a period of time, which makes it difficult to diagnose in adults with the same condition, who can exhibit a certain restlessness. This is the reason why adults with AADHD have problems in organizing their lives into a structured environment and enjoy sustained success in career and personal life, but it can be achieved through time management and proper counseling for the disorder.

Thus, it is important to understand the true nature of the ADHD as being a mental disorder that calls for early, timely and accurate medical help and possible medication that can cure it to the best degree possible to enable the individual diagnosed with it to lead a fulfilling life. There are many girls who are called "tomboys". They frequently exhibit some of the important features off ADHD, like being more involved in physical activities, but not as reckless as the boys themselves. As a result teachers and parents jump to the conclusion that the child has no interest in academics and is basically not organized, but the possibility of ADHD is seldom considered.

Besides the "tomboy" types, the "chatty" girls could also be suffering from ADHD, but remaining undiagnosed. This is a fusion of over-activity and inattentiveness, and is usually touted as socially extrovert. These girls are extremely talkative than being physically active and cannot stop talking even if they are strictly warned.

They also cannot tell stories comprehensively and will stray from their thoughts because of ADHD.

Those whom we call as "daydreamers" could also be suffering from ADHD. They do not draw any attention to themselves and are very quiet in nature. However, their too much being into themselves and not giving any attention to the class is another form of ADHD, contrary to the "chatty" girls. They may show anxiety and depression when given school projects, but cannot finish the projects because of their lack of staying power. This generally goes undiagnosed because the child is thought to be lazy and, parents and teachers fail to identify the disorder in time.

What is fascinating is that many girls with ADHD have quite a high rate of IQ and could be called "gifted". When a child has a high IQ there are no problems in school work, but their lack loopholes get reflected as they mature into adults. Keep in mind that ADHD is not a learning disorder, and patients do not inevitably are poor performers in school. Till high school they can be quite well off, but with mounting pressure and assignments symptoms may become more and more evident.

Well the naughty little boy is there fine, but did we ever spare a thought about the little girl who sits quiet and withdrawn with her mother, one who is overtly polite, terribly afraid to speak out and draws a blank when spoken to? In all probabilities, everyone would fail to guess that she might be suffering from ADHD or the Attention Deficit Disorder.

Difficult as they are, ADHD has some obvious symptoms too. The affected person suffers from distraction, easy forgetfulness and low self-esteem, faces problem in following fast conversations and gets highly disordered with tasks. ADHD and ADHD both can retard mental growth in this that the affected child has to struggle with school work and assignment deadlines, failing to finish things on time. These disorders also rob the child off his/her ability to manage the belongings and to keep track of time.

ADHD Symptoms:

• Lacks vigor, suffers from sloth

• Values others more, respecting theirindividual limits

• Often unassertive or under-assertive

• Too much obedience

• Excessive humbleness and modesty

• Overtly polite and shy

• Avoiding crowd, preferring to stay alone and socially withdrawn

• Not able to open up easily and befriend, although they make a few bonds

Since it is assumed that girls are generally shy, people often overlook the ADHD symptoms in them and they are left untreated. Their outward calm, quiet and politeness are usually to cover up the inner disturbance. ADHD affected girls are emotional and highly sensitive to criticism; but the feelings invoked thus, after being criticized, remain untold. They just carry on with life, struggling silently. Interestingly enough, their ADHD counterparts move forward with absolutely no sign of stress or fatigue and seem totally unaffected by all deterrents in the walk of life. Girls suffering from ADHD cannot withstand stress and usually draw back more into a shell with a belief that they are good-for-nothing and can never do anything right.

Most children have the combined type of ADHD.

Additionally, sometimes, specific signs of ADHD may be present on the surface and at others, a more intense form of this psychological problem may manifest itself in the form of depression, arrested brain development, bipolar disorders or extreme nervousness, but the infrequent or occasional occurrence of a spell of inattentiveness should never hastily be judged as ADHD as it can be an allergic reaction, nutritional deficiencies or even due to environmental sensitivity or even excess caffeine in the diet.

The Naughty Brat Stereotype

The many, and sometimes very varied signs of ADHD are also the reason why many a time physically active and energetic boys are misdiagnosed with having ADHD when they exhibit generally adventurous behavior, short attention spans in school, changing thoughts and high bursts of energy, which are generally associated with ADHD.

The common stereotypes of the naughty brat running out in a crazy fashion or spoiling everything in his way are more misconceptions than the rule for those suffering this neurological drawback and it's not always that simple to spot a child with ADHD even when we think we can do so on an outing. The common misconception of the unruly, bad boy belies the fact that even the withdrawn and silent little girl may be affected equally by ADHD, which manifests itself in various forms.

Since most school-going kids are keenly tuned in to TV programs in the upward range of 40+ hours a week or computer games, it's natural that a lot of energy is saved up so can be easily directed towards activities, not necessarily indicating ADHD.

In order to determine whether the suspected condition is actually ADHD, mannerisms such as high creativity, ideation, being gifted or being visually innovative should be analyzed. This high aptitude in a child suspected of having ADHD must be properly studied, especially for those kids with short attention spans and those displaying agitation frequently.

A child's parents need to be alert and focused on the behavior of their kid in order to accurately look for and find the absolute behavior indicative of ADHD existing in the child so as to get him or her the best treatment through timely, accurate diagnosis.

ADHD And The Girl Child

ADHD in girls is largely overlooked since girls are assumed to be naturally shy and therefore ADHD-er girls can be left untreated for a long time, which is a bad thing.

From quietness that is not actually demureness to excessive humility that is misinterpreted over politeness, ADHD affected girls are very sensitive and react emotionally to criticism, struggling to cope with life in a silent way and oft times, being stressed by this too. However, their ADHD boy counterparts may be considerably less affected by tiredness or stress factors such as caused by criticism and therefore sail through life effortlessly while the ADHD affected girls suffer in silence and sometimes retreat into a shell as a result.

To help a person with ADHD, it is important to understand that girls affected by this disorder are not only emotional, but also prone to being overly impulsive, sensitive and hyper-active whether they are extroverts or introverts. This raises their normal stress levels, which need to be managed through various techniques that can be taught to them to prevent and control the condition from causing them long-term developmental damage or limiting their life as an adult. It is referred to as the revival time to regroup as ADHD-ers attempt to collect themselves after an emotionally turbulent time by way of these methods. Even ever-loving parents can be the cause of sending ADHD affected girls to the deep end with critical examination of their actions and remarks focusing on their mistakes, such as lack of intelligent action, getting low grades, displaying less than ideal behavior or making wrong decisions that do not appeal to the grown-ups, which can all deflate the affected individual. This kind of criticism must be avoided by well-meaning parents as it can be damaging to the ADHD affected girl and a preferable way to dealing with their wards is to offer constructive criticism with advise on practical ways to improve instead of negative commentary that can be damaging to the child's dignity.

Focusing on a girl's particular asset or skill in a particular field or task is preferable to simply criticizing an ADHD affected child as whatever limited enthusiasm and motivation the girl may have is lost as a consequence of feelings of worthlessness that creep in with the criticism of elders. Appreciating finer points, boosting their morale and giving positive feedback on their good performance in school is a better and more effective way to get ADHD affected girls to develop into confident and worthy individuals.

DIAGNOSIS

Children mature at different rates and have different personalities, temperaments, and energy levels. Most children get distracted, act impulsively, and struggle to concentrate at one time or another. Sometimes, these normal factors may be mistaken for ADHD. ADHD symptoms usually appear early in life, often between the ages of 3 and 6, and because symptoms vary from person to person, the disorder can be hard to diagnose. Parents may first notice that their child loses interest in things sooner than other children, or seems constantly "out of control." Often, teachers notice the symptoms first, when a child has trouble following rules, or frequently "spaces out" in the classroom or on the playground.

No single test can diagnose a child as having ADHD. Instead, a licensed health professional needs to gather information about the child, and his or her behavior and environment. A family may want to first talk with the child's pediatrician. Some pediatricians can assess the child themselves, but many will refer the family to a mental health specialist with experience in childhood mental disorders such as ADHD. The pediatrician or mental health specialist will first try to rule out other possibilities for the symptoms. For example, certain situations, events, or health conditions may cause temporary behaviors in a child that seem like ADHD.

Between them, the referring pediatrician and specialist will determine if a child:

Is experiencing undetected seizures that could be associated with other medical conditions

Has a middle ear infection that is causing hearing problems

Has any undetected hearing or vision problems

Has any medical problems that affect thinking and behavior

Has any learning disabilities

Has anxiety or depression, or other psychiatric problems that might cause ADHD-like symptoms

Has been affected by a significant and sudden change, such as the death of a family member, a divorce, or parent's job loss.

A specialist will also check school and medical records for clues, to see if the child's home or school settings appear unusually stressful or disrupted, and gather information from the child's parents and teachers. Coaches, babysitters, and other adults who know the child well also may be consulted.

The specialist also will ask:

Are the behaviors excessive and long-term, and do they affect all aspects of the child's life?

Do they happen more often in this child compared with the child's peers?

Are the behaviors a continuous problem or a response to a temporary situation?

Do the behaviors occur in several settings or only in one place, such as the playground, classroom, or home?

The specialist pays close attention to the child's behavior during different situations. Some situations are highly structured, some have less structure. Others would require the child to keep paying attention. Most children with ADHD are better able to control their behaviors in situations where they are getting individual attention and when they are free to focus on enjoyable activities. These types of situations are less important in the assessment. A child also may be evaluated to see how he or she acts in social situations, and may be given tests of intellectual ability and academic achievement to see if he or she has a learning disability.

Finally, if after gathering all this information the child meets the criteria for ADHD, he or she will be diagnosed with the disorder.

Some children with ADHD also have other illnesses or conditions. For example, they may have one or more of the following:

A learning disability

A child in preschool with a learning disability may have difficulty understanding certain sounds or words or have problems expressing himself or herself in words. A school-aged child may struggle with reading, spelling, writing, and math.

Oppositional defiant disorder

Kids with this condition, in which a child is overly stubborn or rebellious, often argue with adults and refuse to obey rules.

Conduct disorder

This condition includes behaviors in which the child may lie, steal, fight, or bully others. He or she may destroy property, break into homes, or carry or use weapons. These children or teens are also at a higher risk of using illegal substances. Kids with conduct disorder are at risk of getting into trouble at school or with the police.

Anxiety and depression

Treating ADHD may help to decrease anxiety or some forms of depression.

Bipolar disorder

Some children with ADHD may also have this condition in which extreme mood swings go from mania (an extremely high elevated mood) to depression in short periods of time.

Tourette syndrome

Very few children have this brain disorder, but among those who do, many also have ADHD. Some people with Tourette syndrome have nervous tics and repetitive mannerisms, such as eye blinks, facial twitches, or grimacing. Others clear their throats, snort, or sniff frequently, or bark out words inappropriately. These behaviors can be controlled with medication.

ADHD also may coexist with a sleep disorder, bed-wetting, substance abuse, or other disorders or illnesses.

Recognizing ADHD symptoms and seeking help early will lead to better outcomes for both affected children and their families.

How is ADHD diagnosed in Adults?

Like children, adults who suspect they have ADHD should be evaluated by a licensed mental health professional. But the professional may need to consider a wider range of symptoms when assessing adults for ADHD because their symptoms tend to be more varied and possibly not as clear-cut as symptoms seen in children.

To be diagnosed with the condition, an adult must have ADHD symptoms that began in childhood and continued throughout adulthood. Health professionals use certain rating scales to determine if an adult meets the diagnostic criteria for ADHD. The mental health professional also will look at the person's history of childhood behavior and school experiences, and will interview spouses or partners, parents, close friends, and other associates. The person will also undergo a physical exam and various psychological tests.

For some adults, a diagnosis of ADHD can bring a sense of relief. Adults who have had the disorder since childhood, but who have not been diagnosed, may have developed negative feelings about themselves over the years. Receiving a diagnosis allows them to understand the reasons for their problems, and treatment will allow them to deal with their problems more effectively.

Chapter 8: If A Child Is Diagnosed Is Adhd, What Does It Mean?

Scroll back around 30 years. The children who were born back then that displayed signs of impatience, impulsiveness and lack the ability to concentrate were thought to be gifted. These were considered the signs of a potential genius. They were usually given extra work at school or moved up a few classes because it thought that their lack of concentration and impulsiveness were indicators that the work was too easy and did not stimulate them enough.

How times have changed. Nowadays, a child with the symptoms described above would be categorized as a person with ADHD and a treatment program would follow.

ADHD is a fairly new discovery. It is mainly found in younger school boys. A typical candidate of ADHD will most likely be acting on impulse, display boundless energy and have difficulty concentrating when it is needed. It is also said that a high percentage of these children will spend 5 hours or more every day in front of the TV, computer or entertaining themselves with video games.

There are a number of reasons why they display this type of behavior. These factors may be considered quite serious but may not have any bearing on the childs fitness or psychology. To give you an example, behavior often displayed in kids with ADHD could be because of other issues, such as neglect or abuse. This may become apparent when the child is put on the appropriate medication but certain signs continue to be displayed.

ADHD symptoms could also highlight other psychological issues. These could include depression, severe anxiety and bipolar disorder. Yet in some instances, the signs may be far less extreme . These could be problems in certain environments, reactions to an unknown allergy, too much caffeine or a nutrition deficiency.

In conclusion, the parents, teachers and doctor of the child must take any possibility of ADHD seriously. Treatment should only start once a proper investigation has taken place and all other possibilities have been ruled out.

Therefore, the child's parents and teachers, along with their doctors must treat ADD as a serious issue, which should be treated with not only medication but also proper investigation.

Chapter 9: Managing Add And Adhd In Children

As mentioned earlier in this e-book, there is no definite known cause of ADD and ADHD, other than that it may be an outcome of the interactions of genetic, neurobiological, and environmental factors. It would then follow that there isn't any one sure cure for any singular type of ADD and ADHD, whether it's the predominantly inattentive type, the predominantly hyperactive, or the combination of these two types. But there are proven ways of managing the ADD and ADHD. These are important for family members to know so that they could deal with loved ones who have the disorder, children or adults, and help them survive the condition.

For ADD and ADHD-afflicted children, parents should first make sure that they are really dealing with the disorder and not something else. Teachers, too, should help in determining the actual condition, especially because school children now spend most of their waking hours with them. Other medical problems could lead to children being inattentive or hyperactive, like poor vision or hearing impairments. There have been cases when kids just do not get higher grades and teachers thought they really had limited learning potential. Later on, it comes out they could not read well because they just needed eyeglasses. Adequate evaluation should be done and parents should keep on exploring possibilities until they are sure what is wrong with their children.

After having determined that it is definitely a case of ADD and ADHD, parents should now make sure there is a knowledgeable person whom they can consult from time to time. This has something to do now with building your support structure for dealing with your child's condition. That person may be a learning specialist, a guidance counselor, a school psychologist, a child psychiatrist or pediatrician, or anyone who knows about

ADD and ADHD. It is preferable that this person has worked with afflicted kids and could speak plainly about the disorder. Your support structure will also involve your child's teachers, other members of the family, even friends and neighbors who could help ensure that your child gets the necessary sympathy and support to get through the challenges.

One of the main problems that children afflicted with ADD and ADHD experience is the lack of organizational skills. They get lost in what they are doing because they cannot organize internally what they need to do. To remedy this, parents and teachers may have to show the afflicted child the value of organization. This can be done by externally structuring the child's environment. To illustrate how this is done, parents can devise a list that the child could consult when he gets lost in what he is doing. Even repetitive tasks may have to be listed and times given for their performance. This way, the child begins to see structure in what he does every day. Children with ADD and ADHD need constant reminders, previews, explanations, as well as directions and limits to what they do and where they can go or not go. Write them and post them where visible, and support these with verbal reminders.

It would also help to post rules in the house, as done in school most of the time. This is another way of external structuring so that the afflicted child is reminded that rules – and structure – are constant, and that they apply to the home as well as in school. Later on, in adult life, they wouldn't look at rules in the workplace as any different.

When conversing with an afflicted child, make it a habit to always establish eye contact. This will not only tell the child that he needs to pay attention and look at you when you're talking, but can also retrieve the child from a daydream and "bring him back" to reality. Eye contact also can give silent assurance that you are there for him.

Words of encouragement are important in dealing with the child afflicted with ADD and ADHD. Take note of outstanding accomplishments, no matter how small, and tell him about it. Keep him on track and let him know what is expected of him, and give him positive feedback when he does what is expected.

One of the most crucial training techniques for afflicted children is really how you organize and structure his daily or weekly or monthly tasks. It pays to avoid giving him large complicated tasks that may overwhelm him. Breaking down the task into smaller manageable parts can make the child sidestep the emotion of becoming overwhelmed and responding with something like, "I can't do that!" In general, kids with ADD and ADHD can do a lot more than they actually think they can. The child can prove that when big tasks are broken down into smaller ones.

With small children, this technique can work to get rid of the anticipatory frustration when they are faced with seemingly insurmountable tasks. This kind of frustration can sometimes lead to tantrums. With older children, big tasks broken down into smaller parts can help them avoid the defeatist attitude that develops when they constantly fail to perform complicated tasks.

Since children afflicted with ADD and ADHD are often bored with ordinary things, introducing novelty into the child's ordinary day can help get rid of the feeling of boredom. Children, and even adults, with ADD and ADHD love novelty and respond to it with enthusiasm. So try to be unconventional sometimes, and even though managing this disorder involves a lot of "boring" stuff like lists, structure, and rules, being unconventional will often show them that those things don't necessarily go hand in hand with being boring. Every once in a while, have fun and be silly, and have a good time with your child. That will help a lot.

Always watch out for that sparkling moment when your child would exhibit a special ability or talent that he may not be aware he has. Kids who have ADD and ADHD are sometimes more talented and gifted than what they seem. It just needs the right amount of encouragement, the right coaching, for them to show that "special something" that could be more important than all those negative effects of the disorder. This could lead to a more productive and satisfying life for your child.

Chapter 10: The Myriad Of Myths

ADHD have been recorded for more than 100 years. Attention deficit hyperactivity disorder has been widely debated over for the last couple of decades as more and more children are being diagnosed. Some people think people with ADHD are lazy, stupid and lack will power, however ADHD has been recognized by the National Institute of Health and the US department of Education as a biologically based disorder. Most often ADHD is diagnosed in children; however, since 1978 adults have been formally diagnosed with adult ADHD as well. This is undeniable especially since most children who are diagnosed with ADHD will grow up with the same disorder. To better understand ADHD in its entirety you need to understand what is myth and what is fact.

The criteria for an ADHD diagnosis include hyperactivity, inattentiveness and impulsivity. It's certainly the behavior that ADHD kids engage in, but that behavior can be caused by other factors-some of which can be "cured" very easily.

Seven Factors that Mimic ADHD:

1. Lack of Vitamin D

Lack of Vitamin D is at epidemic proportions today. Kids are eating fewer foods enriched with Vitamin D. Very few foods naturally contain significant amounts of Vitamin D. And, sadly, kids are spending less time outdoors in the sunshine-a major source of Vitamin D.

Without enough Vitamin D, kids' behavior can quickly look like ADHD: hyper, not paying attention, acting impulsive. You'll need to see your child's pediatrician to check Vitamin D levels with a simple blood test.

2. Food coloring

Many children are allergic to artificial food coloring, esp. red dye 40 and suffer with the same results as a lack of Vitamin D. Look in your cupboard and refrigerator for every food or candy that is red. If it has red dye 40 in it, restrict your child from this food and candy. See if that helps with the ADHD behavior, (You'll be surprised at how common red dye 40 is, by the way.)

3. Too much TV

Kids are spending 3-4 hours every day watching TV which results in alarming rates of obesity, lack of physical fitness and adhd symptoms. TV also affects attention: the more hours watching TV, the shorter the attention span. Limiting TV often helps with ADHD symptoms.

4. Chronic Stress

Many kids live in a state of chronic stress. Can be a chaotic home life. Can be anxiety about school. Fear, whether you think it's something they should be frightened of or not, also causes stress reactions in the brain. Whatever the cause of stress, it can easily cause behavior that looks just like ADHD.

5. School is too hard or too easy

If children are overwhelmed in school because the work is too difficult or they have a learning disability, the behavioral results will look like ADHD. The reverse is true too for those kids who find school too easy and thus boring. Talking to your child's teacher and testing can often help.

6. Overly-busy schedule

If kids are too busy, have too many outside activities plus school, they can easily become overwhelmed. Their brain responds by an inability to focus and your child either spaces out or runs around in a hyped up state. Cut down on some activities, slow everything down,

7. Lack of sleep

Are they getting enough sleep? Probably not. Researchers are showing that on average kids are getting at least an hour less sleep every night than previously. Too little sleep can affect kids' cognitive abilities, not to mention cause ADHD symptoms.

Many other myths about ADHD still exist. Are there any you still believe?

Fact

Myth

If you have one child with ADHD, all of your children will have it.	Not all children in the same family have ADHD.
ADHD is not a disability.	ADHD is a recognized disability in the Americans with Disabilities Act (ADA) and the Individuals with Disabilities Education Act (IDEA).
Medication is the only treatment for ADHD.	Medication is only one treatment option.
Schoolteachers want active boys on medication.	Schoolteachers want their students to give their best effort.
If a boy is hyper, then he has ADHD.	Boys who are hyper do not always have ADHD. Other things, such as anxiety, can cause

hyperactive types of behaviors. Some boys who have the inattentive type of ADHD are quiet and like to read.

Schools do not know how to teach boys with ADHD.

Schools are becoming more knowledgeable and must provide appropriate accommodations to boys with ADHD.

Only a psychiatrist can diagnose ADHD. Pediatricians, psychologists, neurologists, psychiatrists, and other mental health and medical personnel can all diagnose ADHD.

Psychologists prescribe medication. Only medical doctors such as pediatricians, neurologists, and psychiatrists and nurse practitioners can prescribe medication.

An equal number of boys and girls are diagnosed with ADHD.

More boys than girls are diagnosed with ADHD.

Boys with ADHD want to behave badly.

Boys with ADHD are not able to behave consistently, independently or predictably.

ADHD is a societal fad and will go away.

ADHD has been recognized since the mid-1800s but has been called by different names.

ADHD and ADD are the same thing.

ADHD is an umbrella term that is used in the DSM-IV criteria in place of ADD, a term found in previous DSM editions. ADD was renamed in 1994 by the American Psychiatric Association (APA).

ADHD is not a real problem. ADHD is a lack of willpower.

ADHD is neuro-behavioral developmental disorder. It is a chemical imbalance in the management systems of the brain. ADHD is a legitimate diagnosis by major medical, psychological, and educational organizations using the Diagnostic and Statistical Manual of Mental Disorders. It is also recognized by the NIH and US department of Education as a biologically based chemical imbalance of neurotransmitters in the brain.

ADHD only affects boys.

Boys and girls are just as likely to be affected by ADHD, there is nothing proven that either sex is more likely to be affected.

Approximately 70% of children diagnosed with ADHD will continue to have symptoms up through adolescence and 60% will continue to experience symptoms into adulthood.

Children with ADHD eventually outgrow their condition.

Parenting doesn't cause ADHD. Children with ADHD cannot control the impulses that make them misbehave. They are not taught to act this way; it is the chemistry in the brain. However, some parenting techniques can improve the intensity of the symptoms. Also, ADHD

ADHD is a result of bad parenting.

is neurological and often genetic.

Some children are undiagnosed, or misdiagnosed during childhood. Others can cope with their symptoms as a child therefore not fully experiencing or recognizing their symptoms until adulthood. Therefore diagnosis of ADHD is prevalent and adequate.

You can't have ADHD as an adult if you weren't diagnosed as a child.

Although there isn't a test that diagnosis ADHD in adults, the Diagnostic and Statistical Manual of Mental Disorders and American Medical Association clearly documents and lists

It is impossible to accurately diagnose ADHD in adults.

symptoms of ADHD in both children and adults and medical professionals have specific standards on diagnosing such disorders.

Many people with ADHD have an above average intelligence. However, the imbalances in the brain cause symptoms, which make the person look like they are stupid or lazy. Many legendary people are thought to have had ADHD. People who can successfully manage their disorder have gone on to be CEOs and owners of companies that are still successful today.

People with ADHD are stupid and lazy.

Everyone

ADHD has nothing to do

experiences symptoms of ADHD at some point; intelligent people can overcome these symptoms.

with intellect. Many people with ADHD are very highly intelligent. Everyone can experience the symptoms of ADHD. In people without ADHD it's normally due to over stimulation, attitude, mood, or fatigue. For people who suffer from ADHD they are chronically impaired by their symptoms.

Someone with ADHD can't be depressed, anxious, or have psychiatric problems.

Someone with ADHD is actually 6 times as likely to experience another psychiatric or learning disorder.

ADHD medication causes people to abuse drugs.

The prescription medication used for treatment of ADHD has been proven safe and effective. It is more likely that untreated patients with ADHD have a higher risk to abuse drugs due to addictive tendencies. Treatment reduces the risk.

Chapter 11: What Is It Anyway?

As a parent, a lot of us have spent sleep deprived nights wondering whether our kid is struggling with ADHD. With just cause too, the majority of us know about fundamental results of the condition and clearly shrink at the idea of needing to cope with it. Aside from the worry the disease can be challenging to cope with there's always this subconscious guilt in many parents to be accountable for their kid's problem, the majority of us blame ourselves because of not being strict enough or disciplinarian enough to have straightened out the disorder. While each one of these worries are very normal they aren't always what we might call rational or well-founded.

It appears you will find about 3 broad procedures in the standard growth and development of a young child. The initial one among these is observable in infants. Throughout this time around babies get occupied having a certain object or act and concentrate onto it completely, therefore disregarding almost anything else. When the child's development stalls only at that specific point it could later show indications of autism.

In the second stage, noticed in slightly teenagers, the kid has an interest in a number of things all at one time and they are therefore not capable of focusing on one for over a couple of minutes. When the child stops at this time of development he may later go onto be afflicted by what we traditionally termed as ADHD.

The best stage equips the child's potentials to mature to some extent where they are able to easily and under your own accord point their attention inside a certain direction for any lengthy time period and may alter their selection of direction or their actions linked to it whenever they need or want. This stage therefore is an important transition stage which moulds the kid for achievement within the class and also the real life.

What the majority of us don't know is the fact that ADD doesn't simply make a person not capable of focusing on anything for any certain time period additionally, it makes him/her not capable of determining where they would like to direct their attention as well as for how lengthy. For example, if the ADD sufferer is crossing the street, regardless of being tutored for just like a couple of 1000 occasions regarding how to do this securely he/she is probably to carry out it all of a sudden with no care on the planet in regards to what the status from the visitors are. All they are fully aware, vaguely this too, is that they must mix the street, but after getting appreciated they get rapidly attracted by a few other idea or factor and rapidly to a different, so that when they achieve the other side (which is a reasonably struggle given their reckless behavior) they've most likely worked having a dozen items of ideas already!

Around the opposite finish, ADD also makes people concentrate on some specific object or act so completely they get wholly consumed inside it and therefore are absolutely cut-removed from anything else. They may therefore watch exactly the same film over and over or read a particular page frequently with absolute nonchalance. Later this behavior could easily get molded into habits well over-eating or substance-abuse or compulsive behavior.

Another number of ADD is Attention Deficit Disorder, or Attention deficit hyperactivity disorder, which will keep its sufferers always alert, moving in one spot to another doing something or another not able to unwind, not capable of settling lower. Kids struggling with this could literally drive their parents insane and them up nights, attempting to calm the youngster and set him to rest.

While experience has brought most Researchers to summarize that ADD isn't a problem the kid will outgrow (that's it is not so what can be called self-healing) they also have quite emphatically eliminated any possibility of the parent's become accountable for leading to it. So if your little one is struggling with ADD quit accusing yourself, rather recognize the issue for what it's and phone a professional as quickly as possible.

Chapter 12: Helping Your Child With Schoolwork

Home can be stressful for any student in general. Following are a number of recommendations to overcome difficulties with homework anxiety. Have list of support team. They can be class peers or homework buddies, tutors, school teacher. Create a list of phone numbers and Email addresses for the following:

Online/Private tutor

Homework buddy

Teacher

ADD/ADHD Coach

Create a homework schedule and checklist. Find a place at home that feels comfortable, quiet and is well lit. Student should have a study desk with neat pencil/pen holder, color coded subject folders, colored sticky pads and a current year desk calendar. The desk should be clutter free and may have a plant or inspirational picture or image. One idea is to have folders labeled mail, homework to be done and homework completed.

As a parent, you bear the full responsibility of ensuring that your child will be able to do his or her homework and finish it successfully. For a parent who has a child with ADD/ADHD, patience and understanding is very important. Work daily to create a habit for your child to stay on task. You should spend time helping them accomplish their homework. You should be patient enough to keep on repeating the instructions and make sure that they fully understand the given topic.

a.Allot a specific time for doing homework

There is a good chance that your child will easily remember to do and accomplish his or her homework if you constantly do it at a particular time and place. Making this as a routine will allow your child to remember the task and include it in their everyday life. Make sure that the place where you will be doing the homework is free from clutters and other objects that could potentially distract them from accomplishing the work.

b.Maximize the hour by taking as much breaks as possible

A person's attention span does not normally last for more than 1 to 2 hours. Working in 30 min increments is best to retain information. Keep this in mind as you work out the routine homework time with your child. Take breaks frequently – every 20 to 30 minutes. This will help the students focus and not get distracted.

c. Assist them in organizing work

It may be a very difficult task to do, but you have to do your best to introduce the concept of organization to your child. Doing so will help your child form a routine and easily remember the things he or she is supposed to do. Prepare checklists and initially assist them when they prepare their things for school. This way, they will be able to remember and have a structures routine and list in place. Put all papers, modules and quizzes into color coded folders and envelopes so that they will not get lost.

d.Prepare an extra set of school materials

It was mentioned earlier that people diagnosed with ADD/ADHD often forget things easily due to lack of focus. There is a possibility that your child's materials for school may get misplaced. It would be much better and convenient for both you and your child to have an extra set of schoolbooks, materials and papers. This way, you will be fully prepared.

e. Use examples and analogy when explaining lessons

To help your child better understand a lesson without losing her interest; try to use a lot of examples and analogies. This will help them explore the lesson within the depths of their imagination. Provide examples that they will find amusing and easy to understand. Keep your explanations short and easy to understand so that they will not grow tired of the lesson. Help your child enjoy learning about the topic and create a sense of curiosity in them.

f. Set time limits

Setting a time limit to accomplish a particular task helps the student do their work fast and efficiently. Moreover, setting time limits provides a sense of challenge and adventure to the child, providing excitement and enthusiasm as they exert their effort to finish it within the given time frame. Setting time limits will help the students concentrate on the task and guide them to finish the task given to them properly and concisely.

g.Allow your child to move around during homework time

Studies show that children with ADD/ADHD can work better if they are allowed to move around when doing homework. They are able to retain more information and remember it more as they usually associate these information to the physical activity they were doing at the time that they were studying the lesson. This way, the child will be more comfortable in his environment when attempting to accomplish schoolwork.

h.Read aloud

It was stressed in the earlier parts of the book that people diagnosed with ADD/ADHD easily gets bored. Try to make study session a little more interactive by letting them read out loud. Furthermore, studies show that auditory help from the people surrounding the patient with such disorder retains memory and enthusiasm of the child.

Chapter 13: Adhd And Depression

Attention-Deficit Hyperactivity Disorder (ADHD) is a neurodevelopmental condition that affects children and adults. ADHD develops when the brain and central nervous system develop impairments related to growth and development. A person with ADHD will show varying degrees of these three behaviors: inattention, impulsivity and hyperactivity.

Because children and adults with ADHD struggle with focusing, organizing tasks, and feeling restless, they might experience sadness, guilt, irritability, low self-confidence and helplessness. In some cases, these symptoms can signal depression.

Some experts assert that up to 70% of people with ADHD will seek treatment for depression at least once. One study at the University of Chicago reported that adolescents with ADHD are ten times more likely to suffer from depression than adolescents without an ADHD diagnosis.

Symptoms of Depression

Common symptoms of depression can include:

Depressed mood

Loss of interest in activities once enjoyed

Trouble paying attention and concentrating

Fatigue

Feelings of worthlessness or guilt

Weight loss or gain

Excessive sleep or insomnia

Psychomotor impairment

Thoughts of suicide

Irritability, impulsivity and increased anger in children and teens.

Who Is at Risk?

While boys are more likely to develop ADHD, girls are at higher risk for developing depression with ADHD.3 Children diagnosed with ADHD at a young age is also higher risk. If a mother experiences depression during pregnancy, the child is also at increased risk for ADHD and/or depression.

People with the inattentive subtype of ADHD are also at higher risk for depression compared to those with the hyperactive-impulsive subtype.5

In addition to depression, there is also a risk of suicidal thoughts and actions for people with ADHD. Young females with ADHD are at higher risk for suicidal thoughts, and people with the hyperactive-impulsive subtype may also experience increased risk. A potential side effect of certain medications that treat ADHD is suicidal thoughts. It's imperative that you speak with your doctor if you start to experience suicidal thoughts. If you have a child with ADHD who appears depressed, don't be afraid to ask them if they've thought of hurting or killing themselves, or dying. The sooner you find out, the faster you can find a treatment that is the best and safest.

Getting a Diagnosis

There are some distinctions between ADHD and depression. For example, a depressed person often lacks interest in most activities and motivation, whereas a person with ADHD may have difficult starting a task or organizing one.

A person with ADHD may have low moods triggered by particular events, whereas a person with depression can experience a low mood for weeks or months at a time, often for no particular reason.

The trouble with diagnosing ADHD and/or depression, however, is that there are overlapping symptoms between the two diagnoses. These include feeling of restlessness and having trouble concentrating.

To further complicate things, many of the side effects of ADHD medications, such as sleep problems, loss of appetite, and fatigue, can imitate a depressive episode. This is why it's important to talk to your doctor or a psychiatrist who can help you decipher the exact cause of symptoms. If a child with ADHD experiences sadness, hopelessness, and suicidal thoughts, then this may merit an additional diagnosis of depression.

Treatment Options

ADHD and/or depression are typically treated with medication and talk therapy.8 Psychotherapy, cognitive and behavioral therapy, and psychoeducation can introduce coping skills for symptoms, help build self-esteem, and teach a person to reframe negative thoughts and interrupt destructive behaviors.

Children with ADHD and depression may also benefit from family therapy, so that all family members can understand the diagnosis, help a child manage symptoms, and communicate better with each other. When seeking a therapist, don't be afraid to ask if they have expertise in treating both ADHD and depression.

When medication is prescribed, a psychiatrist or your doctor may choose to treat the disorder with the symptoms that cause the most impairment. Medications and antidepressants may be prescribed together or individually to treat the symptoms. Because some ADHD medications and antidepressants increase the risk of suicidal thoughts, it's important to report all side effects to your doctor.

ADHD TREATMENT

If you or your child has recently been diagnosed with Attention Deficit Hyperactivity Disorder (ADHD), a common neurodevelopmental disorder that causes difficulty focusing, hyperactivity, and impulsiveness, you may be grappling with an array of questions and concerns— including how to navigate the treatment options that exist and what to expect in the coming years.

ADHD Treatment Strategies

For parents hearing that their child has ADHD, the diagnosis can be especially stressful. "Sometimes parents don't know what ADHD is or what it means, which can lead to a lot of misconceptions and fears,"

While ADHD can't be "cured," people of all ages often respond well to common treatment options. For children, whose brains are still developing, how they respond to treatment will be different from adults.

But the good news is that with the right supports in place at an early stage (by school-age), most children's development progresses at about the same pace as their peers who don't have an ADHD diagnosis.

What Is the Best Treatment for ADHD?

Treatment for ADHD for people of all ages should be comprehensive. For kids, this often requires combining pharmacological treatments and occupational therapy. Adults may benefit from a combination of medication and behavioral therapy and/or assistance with organization or structure. Both kids and adults may also sometimes try alternative treatments, as well, to help manage symptoms.

Is It Safe to Give ADHD Medications to Kids?

Parents are often concerned about giving medication to their young children; the latest best practices reveal that not giving medication is a bigger danger than actually giving them for many kids with ADHD.

When children are five or six years old, they typically learn how to focus, how to learn, and how to be successful. Yet kids with ADHD may be challenged because their symptoms can interfere with these typical developmental stages.

That makes getting treatment as early as possible particularly important for kids with ADHD. Right treatment can help relieve some of the distractions and allow normal brain development to progress.

Drugs That Help with ADHD Symptoms

There are several basic categories of medications used today for ADHD.

Stimulants

Stimulants are the most common medications used to treat ADHD. Stimulants target dopamine, which is a chemical in the brain that helps control motivation, movement, and emotional responses. Since kids with ADHD are often hyperactive or overstimulated, it may be confusing to think of giving a child with ADHD a stimulant. But experts explain that by giving a child a stimulant, he or she won't need to seek outside stimulation and will be able to focus and learn. This is important, according to Dr. DeSilva, since this enables kids with ADHD to learn age-appropriate skills and to build important pathways in the brain.

Types of Stimulants

There are variety of stimulants that are used on children. The easiest to tolerate and most effective option for children and adolescents is methylphenidate (which goes by different brand names, including Concerta, Ritalin, Daytrana, Aptensio XR, Metadate CD, Methylin, Quillivant XR).

Other common options include

Amphetamine/Dextroamphetamine (such as Adderall, Adderall XR), Dextroamphetamine (Dexedrine, ProCentra, Zenzedi), and Dexmethylphendiate (Focalin). These short-term drugs can last for about three to six hours and may need to be taken a few times a day.

There are also longer-lasting options (referred to as "intermediate") that work for about 8 to 12 hours, such as Amphetamine sulfate (brand name Evekeo), Methylphenidate (this includes Ritalin SR, Metadate ER, Methylin ER), and Adzenys XR-ODT. Then there are even longer-term options that can work for 12 to 16 hours or longer, including Dexmethylphenidate (Focalin XR), Dextroamphetamine (Adderall XR), Lisdexamfetamine (Vyvanse), Methylphenidate (such as Concerta, Daytrana, Metadate CD, Quillivant XR, Quillichew ER, Ritalin LA).

"Keep in mind that the pharma companies say the medications act for a certain (long) length of time, the actual length of action may be shorter by several hours," "Parents may rely on the provider's experience with these medications for guidance on the length of actual action."

Overnight Option

While most stimulants are given in the morning, a new option of methylphenidate hydrochloride (called HLD200) for kids and adults was also recently approved by the FDA. This new medication is unique because it is given at bedtime for results throughout the following day. Although the premise holds much promise in terms of helping make mornings easier for kids with ADHD, parents should wait until any new medication has been on the market for at least a year before having their children use it.

Concerns about Side Effects

While stimulants can be very effective in children, they also cause some concerns for parents,. For instance, stimulants can be an appetite suppressant which can result in weight loss for adults and can affect the growth of children. So parents should plan ahead to be sure their children are eating enough around the dosing schedule. Making sure kids eat a healthy breakfast that includes protein, such as eggs, before they take their stimulant. During the day while they are on the medication, she suggests providing small snacks and then serving a large dinner.

Other side effects that can occur with stimulants include elevated heart rate and blood pressure, insomnia, and personality changes. If your child has any of these negative effects, it's okay to just stop using it. Gradually weaning your child down is not necessary since these medications are short-acting, and the side effects are temporary. The side effects will cease when the dose wears off.

Addiction and Abuse Concerns

Points out that some parents worry that stimulants can be addictive but points out that the potency of stimulants is 1/10,000 of the potency of recreational drugs. "Nonetheless, college students and others do sometimes abuse stimulants; but actually, children with ADHD who are treated are less likely to abuse drugs than kids with untreated ADHD.

To prevent all kids and teens from abusing drugs, she recommends parents keep the medication in a lockbox and dole out the dose on a daily basis.

Non-Stimulant Medications

While stimulants are the "gold standard" for ADHD, non-stimulant medications are an alternative option for children and adults with ADHD for whom stimulants just aren't a good fit. Non-stimulant medications help to increase a neurotransmitter in the brain called norepinephrine, which can help control attention. Some choices include Atomoxetine (Strattera), Guanfacine XR (Intuniv and Tenex), and Clonidine XR (Kapvay). Many of these come in short- and longer-term versions. They can lower blood pressure and may cause some sedation in some children.

Occasionally, physicians may prescribe hypertension medication (typically used for high blood pressure) to treat ADHD, or antidepressants (commonly used for mood disorders). Both of these approaches can be worth discussing with your child's psychiatrist or pediatrician when more common approaches don't work.

Are ADHD Medications for Adults Different?

Adults typically take the same medication as children and adolescents. Short-term, intermediate, and longer-acting forms of methylphenidates are commonly used.

The right medication for adults is usually determined based on how long symptoms need to be controlled and any side effects the user experiences.

Chapter 14: Ginkgo Biloba For Adhd

A few weeks ago, I discussed the merits of ginseng for treating ADHD. What I did not mention is the fact that this special herb often works even better in tandem with another important "brain herb", Ginkgo biloba. It's benefits also extend beyond the nervous system, and the Ginkgo has been used to treat everything from increasing blood flow to Alzheimer's to glaucoma to hormone replacement to protection against neuronal degradation. While somewhat wary (personally) of using generalized "brain booster" nutrients for ADHD (it is a highly variable disorder of complex etiology and treatment methods), I am interested whenever new research publications arise on the topic. Just this week, a new paper came out on the merits of Ginkgo biloba as an ADHD treatment option.

Irritability is an often overlooked side effect of ADHD. Medications, especially over-prescription with stimulants such as methylphenidate and amphetamines can increase this unwanted side effect. However, Ginkgo exhibited a positive mollifying effect on irritability for the individuals in the study.

While one of the knocks against Ginkgo biloba is that it can sometimes result in sedative effects, the study found these to be extremely mild. However, to go along with the irritability-reducing benefits above, Ginkgo was able to improve the individuals' tolerance for frustration (to the degree that this behavior could be measured).

We have seen previously that oppositional defiant behaviors are often comorbid to ADHD (which can often manifest themselves alongside seemingly unrelated disorders such as auditory processing disorders or even bedwetting). One of the strongest suits of Ginkgo biloba may actually be in curbing these oppositional behaviors. This suggests that Ginkgo may be effective for the more Hyperactive/Impulsive or Combined

Subtypes of ADHD, where comorbid oppositional behaviors are more often seen (as opposed to the predominantly inattentive subtype of the Disorder).

Nevertheless, Ginkgo biloba appeared to boost symptoms of attention and working memory as well. This may suggest Ginkgo's versatility, and that it could be used universally across the ADHD "spectrum", including for the 3 classic or traditional subtypes of the disorder.

The study highlights the relative success for co-treatment with methylphenidate and clonidine for individuals with ADHD and comorbid anxiety disorders. The authors suggest a functional comparison between Ginkgo and clonidine, and hint at its use as an alternative to clonidine/methylphenidate treatment (of course, it is also possible that Ginkgo may be used alongside lower doses of stimulant medications, which could be very useful in reducing unwanted side effects, which are often mild for low doses of stimulants, but typically begin to appear with greater frequency when stimulant dosing is increased). Thus, Ginkgo could possibly act as a side-effect-saving alternative to higher doses of medication.

As a precautionary measure, due, in part to some of its anti-clotting properties, there is some concern about Ginkgo triggering internal cerebral bleeding. Indeed, other studies have also addressed this possible concern, highlighting issues such as haemmorrhage risks, as well as herb-drug interactions with Ginkgo and anti-coagulant medications.

Keep in mind the extremely small nature of the study (only 6 individuals) should be met with healthy skepticism. However, the results were still notable. Statistically significant reductions in some of the trademark ADHD symptoms (fidgeting, restlessness, inattention, etc.) upon Ginkgo biloba treatment definitely highlight its potential as a more "natural" alternative treatment method for ADHD.

The use of Brahmi for Attention-Deficit/Hyperactivity Disorder (ADHD)

Brahmi – History and Background:

The name, Brahmi, is thought to be derived from "Brahma," or creator 10. Since the brain is considered to be the centre of creative activity, the herb which best improves the brain's functioning was called Brahmi.10 Traditionally it was used to anoint newborns, in order to improve their intelligence and "'open the gate of Brahma.'"

This plant is referred to in Sanskrit as Brahmi and in Latin as Bacopa monniera-Folium. It is also known as Jalabrahmi, or "water brahmi." It is a perennial herb found in wet and marshy regions throughout India.15 Sebastian Pole described that Brahmi is a water-loving herb that is a "creeping annual that spreads along banks of rivers as creativity and awareness spread throughout us." Bacopa monniera is the authentic brahmi and is preferred by vaidyas for treatment. Brahmi is often confused with gotu kola, which is also known as brahmi in North

India. Gotu kola's other name is mandukaparni.

The use of Bacopa in Ayurvedic medicine is reported from some sources to date as far back as 3000 BCE 2 and by other sources to approximately the 6th century AD.3 In the classical Ayurvedic text of Caraka, it is classified as medhya-rasayan (medhya: memory enhancing and rasayan: rejuvenating). Caraka described the efficacy of bacopa in treating old age and age-related diseases, promoting memory and intellect, increasing the life span, providing nourishment and improving clarity of voice, complexion and luster. In the Susruta-Samhita, it describes that a three week course of bacopa juice will produce photographic memory and a "person can retain hundred words uttered only twice daily." 15

The Properties of Brahmi

Brahmi has a rasa that is bitter and sweet, virya that is cooling, and vipaka that is sweet. It has a neutralising effect on vata, pitta, and kapha, but in excess can increase vata. It has an affinity for all tissues, especially plasma, blood, and nerve, and for the circulatory, digestive, nervous, and excretory srotas.

The Actions of Brahm

It's Ayurvedic actions include calming vata and redirecting the flow of vata downwards1. It's biomedical actions include that it is a sedative, nervine, cardiotonic, antispasmodic, anticonvulsant, and anti-inflammatory.1 Brahmi is recognised by Ayurvedic practitioners as an adaptogen, an agent that naturally increases one's ability to tolerate physical and emotional stress. It is the "main revitalizing herb for the nerves and brain cells."

Brahmi is one of the main brain tonics used in Ayurvedic medicine. It is regarded as an herb that builds and improves mental performance, improves long- and short-term memory, increases intelligence, increases longevity, decreases senility and ageing, relaxes the whole nervous system, increases circulation to the brain, and stimulates the cerebrovascular system. Brahmi has traditionally been used to improve mental capacity and memory in children.It is attributed with improving learning ability and concentration. It is used for the following disorders: mental disorders, epilepsy, mania and hysteria. It improves the quality of sadhaka pitta, thus influencing one's consciousness. It can be used externally as a head rub for headaches, to clear the mind, as a brain tonic, and to help with hair growth.

Brahmi is considered to be a rejuvenative, particularly to the nervous system. It strengthens the mind and promotes energy as well as sleep; it is often used to treat insomnia. 1 Brahmi is used to help with recovery from exhaustion, stress, and vata imbalance. It is indicated for all conditions with deficient majja dhatu, including Parkinson's disease, Alzheimer's disease, dementia, ADHD, Asperger's syndrome, autism, depression, and drug abuse.

Brahmi is a circulatory stimulant and it accelerates wound healing. It fortifies the immune system by both cleaning and nourishing it. It is very helpful for skin conditions where there is an underlying imbalance in the nervous system. It is also a strong blood purifier

and is used for chronic skin conditions, such as leprosy, syphilis, eczema, and psoriasis. It is helpful for intermittent or periodic fevers, like malaria. It strengthens the adrenal processes involved in carbohydrate metabolism.

Brahmi helps to relieve tension throughout the body, so it is good for constipation and muscle tightness due to stress, as well as menstrual pain. Brahmi leads pitta out of the mutravaha srota, thus it can be used to cool the heat of cystitis and the pain of dysuria. It can be used externally as a medicated oil for joint pain.

Chapter 15: Make Time For Yourself

When it comes to parenting children with ADHD the focus tends to be entirely on them. All of the resources that you find yourself reading focus on what to do with your child, how to reward your child, what kind of consequences to set for your child, etc. However, parenting a child with ADHD is not all about that child; part of the focus needs to be on you as the parent.

One problem that many parents have is they lose themselves in their children. When parenting a child with different needs, it is easy to focus on the child and what is then best for them. What you need to remember is that you as the parent directly influence your child's physical and emotional well being. Everything that you do or say has a direct impact on your child, including the symptoms of their ADHD.

Taking care of yourself is a big part of taking care of your child. When you neglect yourself or your bodies needs, you are going to end feeling run down and tired. These feelings often lead to a lack of patience on your part, which can make parenting even harder than it is. Being impatience might lead you to give in to your child's demands or even give up on the parenting methods that work the best for your child because you simply don't want to deal with things.

Taking care of yourself involves making sure you are getting enough sleep and exercising to keep your body healthy, but that is not all it entails. Keeping your stress levels down is another important aspect of taking care of yourself, when you are under too much stress you lose patience easier, but you also make rash decisions. Find methods that allow you to unwind at the end of a hard day, such as taking a relaxing bath. You can even find ways of dealing with the stress before it even starts, such as mediation.

Parenting a child with ADHD does not mean that you have to do everything on your own. Many parents try to take on the burden of doing it on their own because they feel guilty about asking others to help. The guilt often stems from the fact that ADHD children can be hard to deal with, but it can also stem from the belief that others are judging your skills as a parent. You need to let go of that guilt and ask people for help, it might even come as a surprise in terms of who offers to help.

Accepting help from others is great, but let's face it, they don't know your child like you do. And when you have spent months working on helping your child cope with their ADHD using positive reinforcement and teaching them that their actions have consequences, the last thing you want is for somebody to undo all your hard work. Luckily, spending a few hours with grandma or friends is not going to undo all of the work you have done. If you are worried about how friends or family will handle your child, simply talk to them. Offer them advice on what works for your child and what doesn't. Many times people judge because they don't know or understand, educating them about the unknown will help tremendously.

Another option you have to give yourself a break is to turn to a paid babysitter. This can often bring about feelings of guilt as well; especially if you are a stay at home parent. Dealing with ADHD can be both physically and mentally exhausting, sometimes having somebody to come into your home or even taking your child to a day care center for a few hours a day, can give you that break you need. Those few hours can help you restore your sanity and parents should never feel guilty about that.

Remember as a parent you are not doing this alone, even if you feel like it sometimes. Building a support group that you can rely on is an integral part of taking care of yourself. Your support group gives you somebody to talk to when things seem overwhelming or difficult to handle. Your support group can be an organized group that meets online or in person, or it can simply be your child's doctor or teacher.

Chapter 16: Meditation Techniques

Meditation will definitely help a child with ADHD. If you include techniques of mindfulness and meditation in your schedule for the child, you will notice that it is easier for you to handle him.

Meditation will help the child to be more centred. It will help him to reduce his stress levels and depression. It will also help him to concentrate and focus better.

Start off simple

There are no set rules as to how you should go about dealing with your child's ADHD using meditation. You will have to learn by trial and error. It is important that you start off very slow so that you don't overwhelm the child. You can even start with one minute of meditation practice and increase the duration as you go along. You will also have to work around your child's preferences and nature.

Practice silence

Practicing silence is also a great way to practice mindfulness and meditation. You should dedicate a few hours every few days to complete silence.

Make it fun for the child.

Tell the kid that you are playing a game, in which the one who stays quietest wins. Be creative!

Set rewards so that the kid is interested.

Make sure that this helps the child and does not annoy him.

Accompany your child

You, as a role model, can have a great positive impact on your child. If you lead by example, you make it easier for the kid to follow. You should start meditation and mindfulness practice as a part of your daily routine. Your kid will notice this, and it will be easier for him to inculcate these habits.

Breathing exercises

Breathing exercises are a great tool for the overall development of a child. These exercises will definitely help a child who is battling with ADHD. Breathing exercises will also help you as you move along to help the child.

Victorious breath exercise – The victorious breathing exercise is very simple and easy and will help the child with ADHD to balance out his energies. The breathing exercise will help to calm the child. In this breathing exercise, you should take deep breaths. You need to sit comfortable and take deep belly breaths.

Shining breath exercise- In this breathing exercise, you should sit comfortably and close your eyes. Exhale forcefully from the nose, while keeping the mouth closed. When you exhale, your stomach should go in towards your body. Repeat this as many number of times as possible. Make sure that the child is able to do the breathing exercise comfortably.

Alternate nostril breath exercise – Alternate nostril breath will positively influence the brain. It will balance the right part and left part of the brain, aiding in cognitive ability. In this exercise, you need to hold one nostril and use the other one to inhale and exhale. After a few cycles, this should be repeated with the other nostril.

Yoga

Yoga is a moving meditation technique. You should make yoga as a family ritual. All the family members can spend time together doing yoga. Yoga will help the child to focus on his breath and movements. This is a great way to improve his focus.

Visualization

Another simple way to help the child meditate is to help him visualize. Visualization will help the child enjoy mindfulness.

This can be a great bed time ritual.

You can keep a few minutes aside each night for visualization.

Ask your child to lie down and you should do the same. Ask him to close his eyes.

Ask him how he feels and what is he visualizing.

Take him through the entire process and make it fun. Help him to focus on different parts of his body.

Sing and chant together

A simple way to make mindfulness and awareness a part of your life is to chant and sing with the child.

Set a time for the chanting and singing. Tell the child that it is a fun activity. Keep a watch whether he is having fun or not.

Sing something that the child enjoys.

When you sing together, you help the child to connect with you and also create an atmosphere of being in the present moment.

Chanting will help the child to focus. But, you have to give him his time to enjoy the process.

Once the child is comfortable chanting, ask him to close his eyes. Ask him to focus on how his body feels.

Creative ways to meditate

Meditation is a great way to help kids with ADHD. But, the children can show aversion to meditation. You have to constantly look for ways to keep them interested. You should look at creative ways to include meditation as a part of your child's daily life.

Make the entire practice fun for him.

You can ask him to light a candle and stare at it for a few minutes. This is a simple way to teach them discipline and help them concentrate.

You can make it a part of a game. For example, put a book on your head and walk from one end of the room to the other. After you have done it, ask the child to so the same. When he walks with a book on his head, he will make efforts to not fall and not let the book fall. This is a simple way to bring all his senses to the present moment. This will help him to be more mindful and aware.

Create a simple meditation space for the kid. He should know that the space is meant for something pure and spiritual.

Ask him to bring an object and concentrate on it. Ask him to clean the meditation space. Basically, make him a part of the entire ritual.

Chapter 17: Discipline And The Adhd Child

Keep Calm and Carry On was the catch phrase used by the British government at the beginning of WWII to spur on its citizens. It can also be used as the motto for the parents of children who have ADHD. Parents of ADHD kids walk a fine line between being patient and being a disciplinarian, between allowing your child to develop as far as he/she can and protecting them from the disappointments that you know they will have to face. They all want to spare their children hurt but they also want them to learn to be strong. It is a very challenging job.

Extensive knowledge of the disorder and how it affects your child's functioning can help, when the time comes to discipline your child, because you will be able to discern the difference between conscious bad behavior and behavior that is a result of ADHD. The more you know, the more you can work with your child to reach a happy medium. One rule that never changes, however, is that no matter what the child does or how challenging being the parent of a child with ADHD becomes, you must never withhold love from your child. He or she must always know that they are loved no matter what they do or how they behave.

Discipline techniques used for other children might not work for children with ADHD, but there must be boundaries and codes of conduct established. The kid with ADHD needs a firm but loving hand when being corrected. You must fight to control your anger even when the child is displaying behavior that is clearly unacceptable, or is refusing to follow instructions. Removing privileges such as time playing computer games or looking at television is one way of dispensing discipline. Time outs are also a favorite for parents of children with ADHD. They should be put into effect as soon as the infringement is committed and should not last too long because the child won't be able to complete it, and the effect will be lost. The child is sent to his room or some other previously identified location until they calm down. You also have to be careful not to transfer your frustration at your ADHD child to your other children as they could end up being scolded a lot more severely than they deserved to be simply because you needed an outlet for your anger.

A sense of humor is very valuable in a home with a child with ADHD. You should learn to laugh instead of being embarrassed every time your child does things that might be socially unacceptable in a public place. It won't be easy but try to remember that in time the embarrassment will pass, and all that will be left would be a fun story to relate to your friends and relatives. Sometimes it is okay just to ignore the bad behavior once it is not causing anyone, including the child himself, any harm. This is not suggested as an ongoing way of dealing with the issue of tantrums and other forms of misbehavior, but sometimes it is the right thing to do. Children with ADHD need constant attention and to get it they would be willing to behavior badly because negative attention is still attention. If your child is complaining and arguing for no reason just ignore him until it stops. If the complaining accelerates, let the child know that you would not be responding until he clams down. Like everything else, this will be successful some of the time but won't work in every instance. You will have to gauge when it is the right time to use it.

Your child is going to make many mistakes. Learn to compromise by letting the small ones pass. Pick your battles carefully and deal with issues individually. Don't try to solve every problem at once because that is setting yourself up for disappointment. Through all the challenges, never stop believing in your child and his ability to overcome. Make this clear to the child as well; he should know at all times that you believe in him. Stay positive. Encourage your child to vocalize his feelings. If he is able to tell you when he is feeling sad or angry, you might be able to help him in addressing the problem before it leads to an episode of bad behavior.

Children with ADHD have to adhere to the rules of the family and home they live in just as other children do. Because children with ADHD are often disorganized and impulsive, they need a structured existence even more than others. Make the rules very clear to the child so he knows exactly what is expected of him. Break down instructions into simple steps and speak in the clearest and plainest of ways. Make eye contact with your child when speaking to him so that way you know that he is focused on you and what you are saying. Make him repeat what you said back to you so you know that he has heard it. Many parents have found it helpful to engage in role playing with their child in order to make the link for him between his behavior and the reaction of his parent to it. Children with ADHD can often make that connection and establishing it can help in minimizing behavior that is unacceptable.

These rules may need explaining a bit more often than with other children, so you have to be patient but persistent and keep repeating the limits until they get it. Make the child understand that if the rules aren't followed there will be consequences such as no television or spending time in his room, and if need be those consequences will be implemented.

It is important, however, to remain calm and composed when explaining the rules and when implementing disciplinary measures. Find ways within yourself to also remain calm. Confrontations with your child can be an exercise in patience and tolerance for you and the child. Ensure that the consequences of bad behavior do not cause the child undue distress but are in proportion to the offence. Don't get carried away with the withdrawal of privileges to the point where you are taking away things that are major events in the child's life. Don't say for instance that you are going to cancel his birthday party.

Before you can begin disciplining a child with ADHD, you have to know what behaviors the child can control and which he cannot. Once that is determined you can then decide what the limits of behavior are. Offer rewards to the child for compliance with rules and for following instructions. Discipline for an ADHD child, even more so than an ordinary child, should never involve spanking, beating or any form of violence. Make sure they understand what they did that was unacceptable, and if possible have them redress the wrong, for example, apologizing to another child or cleaning up a mess they made.

Don't try to suppress all the child's efforts at independence. A little defiance might be a positive sign that your child is trying to deal with the world on his own terms. You don't want to take away all his spirit because he is going to need it to cope with the obstacles that he will face growing up.

One of the first things a parent has to learn to do is to censor him or herself. When you are tempted to coddle your child and be his buffer against the world, remember that that child also has to grow and learn to deal with the world on his own. The disorder is not going to go away, it is going to stay with him into adulthood, but at some point in his life you will no longer be there and he will have to be able to fend for himself and get along in the world.

It is important to put structure into the lives of children with ADHD by setting down rules and establishing limits of acceptable behavior. This is especially important if there are other children in the house. Write down the house rules and stick them up somewhere. Make sure that everyone reads and understands them. Try not to be too rigid or to set deadlines and standards that cause rebellion and confrontation. Still give your child a feeling of independence albeit within boundaries.

Although parents should expect some disobedience as with any child, there must be consequences when the child does not follow the rules. Don't assume that his behavior is because of the disorder and cannot be controlled. Although most of the time this will be the case, children with ADHD, like other children, will push as far as they can until their parents stop them. Sometimes unacceptable behavior is deliberate. Stick to your guns. It will probably take longer to get your child with ADHD to comply with your structure than the average child, but you must not give up on them or on the schedule that you have set. Even playtime can be used as a learning tool if used correctly. Use puzzles and other brain stimulating toys when you play with your child. This way he can be learning while enjoying play and spending time with a parent all at once.

Even though you have to instill discipline in your child's life, try to minimize negative feedback and comments. Chances are the child gets enough negativity in his daily life already. Try to teach the way to do things using as much positive and as little negative reinforcement as possible. Any improvement in behavior must be loudly applauded. If the only time that the child gets any attention is when he does something wrong and the rest of the time he is ignored, he will continue to do the wrong thing. Let him know that good behavior can bring him lots of attention too and even better if it is positive attention. When correcting your child, be sure to explain in the plainest terms exactly what he has done that is wrong and why it is wrong. Of course this is easier said than done.

After telling your kid numerous times not to leave his skateboard on the stairs but to put it away in the closet under the stairs, if you almost trip over it as you come down the stairs on your way to work, it is very easy to lose your temper and to begin shouting. Try however to think ahead to what the outcome of that might be. You'll shout and the child will respond by either being crushed or being defiant and shouting back. If he's defiant, that will increase your anger, there'll be more shouting from both sides and general bad behavior will ensue most likely ending with a timeout for the child.

You will feel guilty because you lost your temper and shouted and because you can't seem to get him to carry out what is a very simple instruction. Meanwhile, the skateboard will still be on the stairs waiting to trip someone.

So instead of going through all that, rein in your anger, sit your little one down and explain to him why leaving it there is dangerous, and why there must be consequences to his failure to remember to put it away. Make sure that he understands the issue; keep explaining until he gets it. Walk him through what could happen if someone slips on the skateboard then have him put it away and show how the accident can be avoided just by doing that. This way he can get a clear picture of the consequences of his action either way so he will be more likely to remember the next time.

Do not under estimate the importance of presenting a united front when it comes to discipline. Both parent must agree on the house rules and be consistent in how they are applied. If the parents appear to be divided, the child will pick up on it and use it to his advantage. If you have disagreements on how the rules should be administered, you should have them in private away from the child's hearing and appear before them united. Failure to do this can and often does result in bad behavior in children and teen. This is true even for families where the parents are divorced and custody is shared. If one parent is establishing rule and setting up activity roster but when the child goes to the other parent for the weekend it "anything goes", this is going to result in big problems. So even if you and your spouse find it difficult to agree on much, which is often the case after a divorce, get together and come up with a joint plan for how your child with ADHD is going to spend his time, and how the routine is going to be followed or everyone will suffer. For some parents admittedly, this is going to be extremely difficult and might require the help of a professional. In a world where everything seems to be unpredictable, the child with ADHD must believe that his parents can be depended on to behavior in a predictable fashion.

Chapter 18: Strategies At Workplace Or School For Overcoming The Adhd Challenges

Employers want employees who can focus on their work and have a meticulous and methodical approach with a capacity for speedy work. These qualities are conspicuous by their absence in the adults with ADHD. They are restless, fearful and unsure of themselves and can get easily distracted. They have no correctly structured sense of time or various activities. So, it is difficult for them to retain their job. But, that doesn't mean the patients with ADHD cannot excel in studies and their career. It may be difficult for them, but surely not impossible. Here are a few ways that will help you improve your effectiveness at school or work and boost your performance.

Improving competency

Medication therapy, guidance from experts, meditation, relaxation techniques, a job that you will be interested in, a job that does not demand too much from you physically and mentally, flexible working hours, quiet working conditions and helpful colleagues: all of these would make up a perfect combination that can make it possible for the adults with ADHD to reach the competency levels acceptable to their employer. But, not all the adults affected by ADHD will find such positions. They can think of taking up independent services that they can handle confidently and comfortably.

Steps that help to retain job

ADHD adults can discuss with their boss the needs of their condition and get their help. Keep a planner and refer to it constantly, write down the points discussed with the colleagues, plan regular breaks for you to recoup, set achievable goals and be happy with what you achieve. These tips will surely help you retain your job and slowly climb the ladder of success towards a higher position.

Improvement in school performance

ADHD children will have a lot of difficulties in their school. They fare better when they set a daily classroom routine, have all the rules clearly mentioned on a classroom wall and can refer to the lessons displayed on the blackboard. They can be given the sense of a structured life by providing them a timetable, lists, deadlines and frequent and regular reminders.

Development of executive functions

Executive functions need having a good memory, the ability to reason out the things and a flexibility in approach, planning, execution and solving of problems. ADHD children have to be trained to master these to some degree with the help of experts. They have to be trained to analyze the problems, evolve a workable plan to solve it with the help of a coach, learn to organize everything necessary to put the plan into action, develop different solutions for the same problems, learn to adjust and modify their solution to a changing problem, and complete the task with single-minded determination without allowing anything to distract them. The development of these management capacities will help the child as well as the adult affected by ADHD.

Time management

Time management does not come easily to the persons affected by ADHD. They have to be put through regular practice sessions to be able to estimate broadly the time needed for a small number of elementary tasks like drawing a simple sketch, writing a few paragraphs, finishing lunch or walking from the classroom to the workshop. They should be persuaded to use a clock as often as they can. They should be given a few minutes to perform an activity and the alarm should be set for that time so that they get an idea of how time flows.

A quick start

ADHD-affected persons have to be trained to be able to start on a job as soon as they have it. This is one of the most difficult tasks for them and they should be trained every day to begin their work quickly on any given activity. They should also be encouraged to look back at what they have done in the previous hour and record it so that they can have some clarity about the task and the time and the organization needed to do it.

Accept children as they are

The parents of an ADHD child have to first accept the limitations of the child. They have to recognize the other hidden skills or capacities of the child, learn to respect them and help the child to develop their skills and use them fully. Each child has some strengths. The parents have to try and focus on them and motivate the child to achieve the best with them.

Love and understanding

Often, the child may not be in a position to use these capabilities and perform some elementary tasks. The parents must not lose heart and patience at such time. They have to display understanding, love and empathy for the child in such difficult phases and urge the child to perform even simpler tasks so that the child gains confidence and is able to learn and perform more complex jobs in the future.

Curb impulsiveness

ADHD persons are hyperactive and impulsive. These symptoms can take many forms from reasonable to dangerous or offensive behavior. They tend to let out some remarks they will be sorry about immediately afterward. Adults with ADHD are usually able to curb their impulsive traits. However, the habit must be cultivated in the child by explaining him the consequences of such actions with great patience and empathy.

Counter-measures

The best way to control the impulsiveness involves regular treatment and medication, understanding ADHD and its effects in one's own practical life, being attentive to everything that is happening in the present, noting down the effects of their actions and remembering them, countering the negative thoughts with something positive as soon as they occur to you, taking steps that will make it difficult for you to act impulsively and learning to relax with a calming activity at the first sign of an impulsive behavior.

The life cannot be easy for the persons affected by ADHD. It is equally difficult for the parents of the ADHD-affected children. It is highly recommended for the parents to learn everything about ADHD and handle the child or the grown-up person with love, trust and understanding so that the child responds by doing his best, realizes his true potential and excels in something he is interested in.

Chapter 19: Understanding Behavioral Therapy

Behavioral therapy has been revealed to be extremely effective in treating the symptoms of ADHD in children. This type of therapy is also considered a successful complementary treatment for kids who are taking stimulant ADHD medications, allowing them to receive the latter in lowered doses.

Three Is It

Three approaches are included in treating ADHD in kids using behavioral therapy:

1. Parent Training Approach

In this behavioral therapy approach, parents are taught about their children's condition and the different techniques for managing ADHD behaviors. Although it is known that children with ADHD have difficulties controlling their impulses, listening attentively, and following through on tasks, parents still expect that their kids will show improvement in all these areas.

This means that parents do not have to discipline a kid with ADHD differently from his siblings. It does mean that they have to discipline more frequently and more consistently. Parents of a child with ADHD need to keep in mind that it can take longer for a lesson to sink in, which gives them the feeling that they have to parent their kid five times.

Parent training approach includes the time-out and rewards/consequences methods:

Time-Out Method:

1. Differentiate time-outs from time-ins. For example, if your child hits his brother and you put him in time-out as a consequence, make sure you have praised him previously for having played without trouble with his brother. It is also important that you praise your child after his time-outs for proper behavior and good attitude. Your kid will fail to realize the consequences of his actions if he does

not see the contrast between time-outs and time-ins.

2. Make sure to stay calm. In case your kid ignores you after telling him that you are placing him on time-out, let him know you are adding an extra minute to the time-out period. If he still resists going to time-out, extend his time-out by another minute. If he still ignores you after having done that, fight the urge to pick up your child and then drag him to his time-out area. Doing so will only worsen the situation. Plus, the negative attention he receives for his behavior will only reinforce it, even if your kid does it unintentionally.

Try setting a timer as a prompt or signal that his time-out is about to start and that it is about to end. In case your child does not cooperate, let him know the time-out cannot begin until he quietly goes to his time-out area.

3. Ensure that your child's time-outs are short and relevant to the issue at hand. Otherwise, your child's time-outs could easily turn into a series of battle-of-the-

wills. Expect a young child to feel that one to two minutes of time-out period is quite long. On the other hand, a preschooler may think he could get away with a thirty-second or one-minute time-out period if he stays quiet in his time-out spot.

A better way of making sure your child sees that his time-out is a result of a misbehavior is to impose a consequence that matters a lot to him. An example would be to keep him from playing his computer games for the day. It is important that you never give in if he tries to bargain with you or badger you into lifting the consequence you have imposed.

4. Practice giving your kid time-outs. Let him pretend to misbehave, then tell him you are sending him to his time-out spot for a certain period of time. Make sure to avoid giving him a chance to fight with you when practicing his time-outs.

Rewards and Consequences Method:

Use positive reinforcement (giving specified rewards) when your child shows desired behaviors, and use unwanted result/punishment (giving consequences) when he fails to meet certain goals.

1. Instead of toys or his favorite food, use enjoyable activities, praise, and privileges as rewards for your child.

2. Create a chart for awarding your kid's good behavior, then fill it with stars or points accordingly. The chart will be his visual reminder for his successes.

3. Remember that each good behavior should always come with a reward.

4. Make sure to frequently modify the rewards you give to your kid, as more of the same reward can get him bored.

5. Keep in mind that while giving immediate rewards produces better results than promising your child a reward in the future, giving small rewards that lead to the big one does work as well.

6. Spell out the consequences for misbehavior in advance. Follow through with consequences immediately after your kid does misbehave.

7. Keep your kid away from environments and situations that trigger misbehavior.

8. As your child what he could have done as an alternative when he misbehaves. Encourage him to demonstrate it.

2. Child-focused Approach

This behavioral therapy approach involves helping your child with ADHD develop different skills that they need to succeed in life, such as problem solving skills, academic skills, and especially social skills.

Children with ADHD usually have trouble navigating simple social situations, which is worsened by the fact that they often struggle with issues of low self-esteem. This is where social skills training comes in handy for kids with ADHD. Social skills training is usually done in group settings, wherein a therapist takes the lead and gives demonstrations on what behaviors are appropriate for different social settings. The kids are then asked to practice repeating what the therapist has demonstrated. This training allows kids with ADHD to learn to read into other people's reactions so that they can behave in more acceptable ways.

Improving Your Child's Social Skills At Home

Learning social skills and knowing how to navigate different social rules can be challenging for kids with ADHD. Follow these tips on helping him develop better listening skills, learning to read facial expressions and gestures, and having better interactions in social situations:

In a gentle but honest manner, let your child know about his challenges and the changes he can make.

In the matter of selecting playmates for your kid, be careful to choose those with physical and language skills that are similar to his.

In the beginning, keep invitations for having your kid's friends over down to one or two. Pay close attention to them while they are playing. Don't tolerate any yelling, pushing, and hitting.

Have role-playing sessions with your kid, in which you act out different social scenarios. Make sure to frequently trade roles and to have fun in the process.

Make it a priority to let your child play and to reward him often for showing good behavior while at play.

3. School intervention approach

The school intervention approach in behavioral therapy treatment of ADHD in kids involves helping teachers meet their educational needs by managing ADHD behaviors inside the classroom.

Your child's condition obviously gets in his way of learning – he can hardly absorb a lesson and he can leave his work unfinished because he is either busy tuning out what he should be listening to or he is too preoccupied with jumping around the classroom. And all of these should not be a surprise, as the things your child has to do in school – listening quietly, sitting still, concentrating, and following instructions – are the same things that they find quite challenging to do. The reason is not because they do not want to do these things, but because they cannot do these things.

But your child with ADHD has all the right to achieve success in school, with the combined help of his parents and teachers. Here are different strategies you can try:

Ask your child's teacher to:

1. Find ways to lessen potential distractions in the classroom. It would be preferable to always seat kids with ADHD, especially those who have difficulty focusing, near the teacher. The teacher may also stand near the student while giving out directions; this way, there are less barriers and distractions for the student to overcome in absorbing what is being said.

2. Make room for movement. Let your child fidget in his seat or move around the classroom by setting up reasons for them to move. It would be great to give kids with ADHD the opportunity to get drinking water, do an errand for the teacher, make

a trip to the bathroom, or any other task that requires physical action. The teacher may also let a child with ADHD keep a squeeze ball or another small object in his desk, which he can quietly manipulate without distracting his classmates.

3. Make way for transitions. Ask the teacher to remind your child about an upcoming task or activity, be it recess, next class, or time for another book. It would be great if the teacher also gives lots of reminders and advance notice for field trips and other special school events. Before the day ends, the teacher may also help your kid prepare to go home by reminding him about the items he needs to accomplish his homework.

4. Allow for some playtime. It helps to let your child enjoy his free time during recess instead of using it for working on a missed assignment, as playing during recess actually helps him improve his focusing ability.

Be Your Child's Teacher's Partner:

1. Engage in regular communication with your child's teacher about his difficulties.

2. Assist your child as he organized his papers before doing homework and before heading for school the next morning.

3. Check if has finished his homework in subjects that has difficulties with, especially if he is on the brink of failing in class.

4. If necessary, make a request for the teacher to use a daily/weekly report.

5. Make sure your kid's ADHD medication is doing what it is supposed to do when your kid is in school and while he does his homework.

6. See to it that your child places his finished homework in the right folder/organizer.

7. Until the school semester ends, make sure to save all of your child's completed homework.

Turn Learning Into a Fun Activity:

1. Use physical motion when introducing a lesson in class.

2. Make up silly songs to make the details of a new lesson easier to keep in mind.

3. Make dry facts more interesting and more likely to be remembered by connecting them to trivia.

Make Math Enjoyable:

1. Play games that make numbers so much fun for your child. You can play dominos, dice, and memory cards to make math enjoyable for your kid, or you might just wiggle or tuck in your fingers as you help your kid add and subtract.

2. Make up silly acronyms. These will help your child remember the math rules on operations, divisibility, etc.

3. Draw illustrations that can help your child have a better understanding of different mathematical concepts, such as word problems.

Make Reading Irresistible:

1. Read to your child and make sure to make reading time cozy for both of you.

2. Act out what you just read together. Allow your child to pick his preferred character in the story to act out. Ask him to pick your own character as well. Bring the story to life by using costumes and amusing voices.

3. Make bets with your child. Ask him constantly about how he thinks the story will unfold. For example, say "The boy in the book sure seems courageous; I bet he will be the one to save the whole town!"

Getting Things Organized:

1. Set up a folder to hold all of your child's completed homework. It would be a great idea to organize loose files in color-coded folders and to demonstrate to your child the proper way of filing.

2. Have extra sets of school materials and textbooks at home, if possible.

3. Assist your child in organizing his belongings in his backpack, pockets, and folders every day.

4. Teach your child how to make checklists, then help him learn how to use them. Remind him to cross off an item as soon as he accomplishes it.

Getting Homework Done:

1. Establish a specific place and time for your child to do his homework. Get rid of the TV, pets, and other possible distractions.

2. Use timers and an analog clock in teaching your child about the course of time. These devices will also help you monitor how efficient your child is in doing his homework.

3. Let your child take a break from doing homework every 10 to 20 minutes.

Chapter 20: Do You Have Adhd? Diagnosing For Adults

Chapter three details the complicated process that must be carried out to properly diagnose a child with ADHD, but it isn't usually that complicated for adult sufferers. You will not have to take forms to your boss or have your friends report their experiences of your behaviors. You are mature enough to properly report your own symptoms and tell your doctor how those symptoms are affecting your daily life.

The problem with diagnosing this disorder is that there is no standard test that can say whether you have the disorder or not. There are tests that have been developed to help in diagnosis, but they are not standard tests that automatically reveal who is suffering and who is not.

Some adults are diagnosed after working with a therapist or psychiatrist for a brief period of time. Symptoms are discussed and the therapist is able to talk more with the patient to determine whether those symptoms are related to stress and other factors, or ADHD. Treatment is then applied to treat the symptoms, whether an official diagnosis is delivered or not.

When this disorder is treated for adults or children, it is only the symptoms that are treated anyway. There is no way to cure ADHD. It is helpful for children to be given an official diagnosis so they can receive special treatment at school and can be assisted by parents to overcome their limitations.

In adulthood, that diagnosis is not as important. What matters is that you receive the treatment you need so you can overcome your limitations and be as successful in life as possible. You can receive that treatment after talking with your doctor about your symptoms or working with a therapist or psychiatrist.

Is the Sign on the Wall?

If you are seeing signs that you believe signal you have ADHD, you may be experiencing some or all of the following:

You daze off during meetings and struggle to keep up with what is happening around you.

You are easily distracted and find it difficult to focus on one thing when other things are happening around you.

You require a lot of sensory stimulus to focus, such as having a television on in the background while you do paperwork.

It seems impossible for you to remain organized, and that affects your life negatively.

Your house is a mess and you find it difficult to manage, prioritize and organize your home life.

You have an impulsive tendency that sometimes makes you less responsible than you should be at your age.

This is just a short list that reflects how many adult sufferers are experienced on a daily basis. If you relate to some of these statements, it may be time to see a medical professional to have symptoms treated. Keep reading this book to educate yourself on potential treatment options.

Chapter 21: Set Up A Simple Money Management And Bill Paying System

Establish an easy, organized system that helps you save documents, receipts, and stay on top of bills. For an adult with ADD/ADHD, the opportunity to do banking on the computer can be the gift that keeps on giving. Organizing money online means less paperwork, no messy handwriting, and no misplaced slips.

Switch to online banking. Signing up for online banking can turn the hit-or-miss process of balancing your budget into a thing of the past. Your online account will list all deposits and payments, tracking your balance automatically, to the penny, every day. You can also set up automatic payments for your regular monthly bills and log on as needed to pay irregular and occasional ones. The best part: no misplaced envelopes or late fees.

Set up bill pay reminders. If you prefer not to set up automatic payments, you can still make the process of bill paying easier with electronic reminders. You may be able to set up text or email reminders through online banking or you can schedule them in your calendar app.

Take advantage of technology. Free services such as Mint and Manilla can help you keep track of your finances and accounts. Both services take some time to set up, but once you've linked your accounts they automatically update. Manilla consolidates your statements and bills from all of your accounts into one place. Mint tracks all of your bank account and credit card transactions, and also offers budgeting and other financial analysis tools. Both tools can make your financial life easier.

Get organized at work

Organize your office, cubicle, or desk, one manageable step at a time. Then use the following strategies to stay tidy and organized:

Set aside daily time for organization. Set aside 5 to 10 minutes a day to clear your desk and organize your paperwork. Experiment with storing things inside your desk or in bins so that they don't clutter your workspace as unnecessary distractions.

Use colors and lists. Color-coding can be very useful to people with ADD/ADHD. Manage forgetfulness by writing everything down.

Prioritize. More important tasks should be done first. Set deadlines for everything, even if they are self-imposed.

End distractions

Let your workmates know you need to concentrate, and try the following techniques to minimize distractions:

Where you work matters. If you don't have your own office, you may be able to take your work to an empty office or conference room. If you are in a lecture hall or conference, try sitting close to the speaker and away from people who chat mid-meeting.

Minimize external commotion. Face your desk towards a wall and keep your workplace free of clutter. To discourage interruptions, you could even hang a "Do Not Disturb" sign. If possible, let voicemail pick up your phone calls and return them later. If noise distracts you, consider noise-canceling headphones or a sound machine

Save big ideas for later. All those great concepts that keep popping into your head? Jot them down on paper for later consideration.

Stretch your attention span

As an adult with ADD/ADHD, you **are** capable of focusing—it's just that you may have a hard time keeping that focus, especially when the activity isn't one that you find particularly engaging. Boring meetings or lectures are hard on anyone, but for adults with ADD/ADHD, they can be a special challenge. Similarly, following multiple directions can also be

173

difficult for those with ADD/ADHD. Use these tips to improve your focus and ability to follow instructions:

Get it in writing. If you're attending a meeting, lecture, workshop, or another gathering that requires close attention, ask for an advance copy of the relevant materials—such as a meeting agenda or lecture outline. At the meeting, use the written notes to guide your active listening and note taking. Writing as you listen will help you stay focused on the speaker's words.

Echo directions. After someone gives verbal instructions, say them aloud to be sure you got it right.

Move around. To prevent restlessness and fidgeting, go ahead and move around—at the appropriate times in the right places. As long as you are not disturbing others, taking a walk or even jumping up and down during a meeting break, for example, can help you pay attention later on.

Exercise and spend time outdoors for adult ADD/ADHD

Working out is perhaps the most positive and efficient way to reduce hyperactivity and inattention from ADD/ADHD. Exercise can relieve stress, boost your mood, and calm your mind, helping work off the excess energy and aggression that can get in the way of relationships and feeling stable.

Exercise on a daily basis.

Choose something vigorous and fun that you can stick with, like a team sport or working out with a friend.

Increase stress relief by exercising outdoors—people with ADD/ADHD often benefit from sunshine and green surroundings.

As well as relieving stress, relaxation exercise, such as meditation, yoga, or tai chi, can teach you to better control your attention and impulses.

Get plenty of sleep for adult ADD/ADHD

Sleep deprivation can increase symptoms of adult ADD/ADHD, reducing your ability to cope with stress and maintain focus during the day. Simple changes to daytime habits go a long way toward ensuring solid nightly sleep:

Avoid caffeine late in the day.

Exercise vigorously and regularly, but not within an hour of bedtime.

Create a predictable and quiet "bedtime" routine.

Take a hot shower or bath just before bed.

Stick to a regular sleep-wake schedule, even on weekends.

Eat right for adult ADD/ADHD

Eating healthfully can reduce distractibility, hyperactivity, and decrease stress levels dramatically.

Eat small meals throughout day.

Avoid sugar as much as possible.

Eat fewer carbohydrates, while increasing your protein intake.

Chapter 22: Build Socializing Into Your Schedule

That way, your desires to meet new people, have interesting conversations, and keep up with friends are taken care of automatically. Take a class, join a book club or a lecture series, or start a dinner club.

It is very easy to neglect going out and living life. Especially when you are hyperfocused on something. If you put it into your planner, you will never have to worry about it. You don't have to be a social butterfly and constantly be on the go. But you need to take the time to care for your relationships. They take work and it's easy to forget about them with ADHD.

If you have to force yourself to go to dinner, or a friends house once a week that's fine. You have to socialize to lead a healthy lifestyle. Once or twice a week do something out of the house other than work. You will be surprised how much better you feel afterwards.

Pre-assemble Clothes Into Complete Outfits

Pre-assemble your clothes into complete outfits. You can have all of your outfits in your closet and ready to go. This way you won't have to worry about having something to wear. You won't have to worry about picking something. I have spent too many precious minutes before work, looking for something to wear.

Doing it this way allows you to just grab a hanger with an outfit already on it, ready for the day. I personally even go as far as to have whatever I need in my pockets before I go to sleep. I will put my keys and wallet in my pants. With my belt already looped. So when I wake up, I just throw on my pants and I don't have to worry about my keys and wallet. I take a shower at night. All I have to grab is my phone, brush my teeth and I'm out the door.

This has really helped me only worry about the day ahead of me. It allows me to start my day on the right foot, even if I wake up a little later than I should have.

Deal With Problems Now

Deal with a problem as soon as it happens. All of us with ADHD are known to procrastinate and let things pile up. If you have to return a phone call, just do it.

I am a firm believer that if a task takes less than 5 minutes, just do it. If there is one bag of trash to take out, just take it out. Because before long, there will be 3-4 trash bags that have piled up. You turned a 2 minute task into something that now will take 10-15 minutes. If you always do this you won't have to worry about doing it later.

Wash your dish as soon as you eat. That way you never have to wash dishes. You will never have to worry about a sink full, if you always have them washed. If you need to mow the lawn on a Saturday morning. Just go do it and you will have the rest of the day. If you don't do it, it will be on your mind all day and you won't enjoy it anyway.

If you are already passed this point and things have piled up. This is the same way you can fix it. Use our guideline for turning big tasks into smaller ones. When you do get caught up, take dealing with a problem now seriously.

Prioritize

Decide what tasks are most important. Take a minute and figure out a list. Go from highest priority to lowest. Once you have your list work from top to bottom. Take it one step at a time. Once again, this comes back to turning big tasks into smaller tasks.

You can prioritize one task into smaller tasks to make it easier. While you are doing this, have your timer running so you stay on task. Get a watch if you have to, so you don't always have to look at your phone. Bringing your phone out is another chance for you to lose focus. We really have to watch the clock with ADHD. It is too easy or us to lose track of time, and let things pile up. It also shows us if we are losing impulse control or not.

Sometimes it feels like we have been at a task for hours, and we have only been at it for a few minutes. Timers are so important for this reason. It works both ways for keeping us focused, and also not letting us get unfocused.

Chapter 23: Benefits Of Adhd

Two thirds of patients prescribed ADHD medication stop taking it within a year. Patients discontinue their drugs for all kinds of reasons including side effects, mistrust of pharmaceutical manufacturers or of the medical care system, costs, etc., but other patients and parents discontinue because of issues regarding the long term security and benefits of ADHD drug treatments.

Those of us with children on stimulant medication have nagging anxieties about the long-term brain changes brought about by ADHD drug treatment, the brain changes that will continue into adulthood, and about whether these long-lasting brain changes will be advantageous or not. There is little disagreement, about the long term effects of not treating ADHD, in the medical community. Researchers and medical providers or all specialties concur that ADHD should be diagnosed and treated immediately. The basis for this unanimous decision is linked to the findings from research studies that have followed people with ADHD over long intervals of time. These studies, called longitudinal studies, are hard and not cheap to perform but the findings from these studies also carry an excellent deal of weight.

There have been several longitudinal studies looking at what happens to untreated kids with ADHD when they reach maturity. The results of these longitudinal studies have consistently revealed that untreated ADHD leads to increased dangers of:

Poor academic outcomes

Poor job related results

Mood disorders

Addictive ailments

Youth and Young Adult delinquency

Despite an understanding of the negative dangers associated with non-treatment, many patients and parents have concerns regarding the long-term hazards along with the long term benefits of drug therapy. The loudest voiced concerns involving risks include questions about stimulant treatment and:

· Increased Cardiac Difficulties

·Weight/Height abnormalities, and

· Increased Illegal drug use

The majority of longitudinal studies performed looking at these three specific risks have found there are no long term cardiac hazards in the use of ADHD stimulants, that stimulant use may, actually, lower not increase the threat of illegal drug use, and that stimulants do cause modest reductions in weight and bone development.

The question of academic success and ADHD drug treatment is more uncertain. While it's clear that not treating ADHD results in more academic failure. There's little persuasive evidence that patients which are treated with drug therapy fare considerably better. A longitudinal review study looking at nearly 9000 patients with

ADHD found that long-term drug use was correlated with modest improvements in standardized test scores but the signs for long term improvements in school grades and grade retention was convincing.

Other questions such as whether the stimulants permanently alter the size or connectivity of the brain, whether the stimulants empower brain plasticity changes which might be advantageous in the long-term and whether stimulants cause permanent genetic or epigenetic changes which are harmful or beneficial are harder to reply. Some animal and human longitudinal studies have suggested that there are genetic changes that result from ADHD drug treatment or long-term neurological but other studies have indicated just the reverse.

Compliance with ADHD drug treatments will merely improve once patients and parents have replies with their nagging issues about the long term brain changes brought about by ADHD drug treatment and about whether these brain changes that are permanent will be advantageous or not.

Chapter 24: Alternative Approach Provides Help For Children With Adhd

Powerful help for children with ADHD is as of now one of our most critical difficulties today. Creative critical thinking and initiative abilities are required more now than any time in recent memory. Numerous children and adolescents with ADHD are skilled with a capacity to get to a virtuoso level of insight, yet may require some assistance in learning viable approaches to outfit and channel the abnormal state of creative vitality that is accessible to them.

Since a child's initial condition significantly affects all levels of improvement, each instance of child ADHD exhibits profoundly singular symptoms which require a customized plan of activity for successful treatment.

Section of the "No Child Left Behind Act" of 2001 (NCLB) has teachers, understudies and guardians under weight to push understudies through inflexible educational modules. Understudies who aren't ready to stream with the structure are ordinarily named as ADD/ADHD and put on stimulant drugs to make them simpler to oversee and more like "ordinary" children.

Children under 16 are being put on ADHD physician recommended drugs at an expanded rate of over 33% since 2005. Ritalin and Concerta are two of the more well known stimulant medications that work to some degree by smothering alpha mind waves, which are transcendent in many "skilled" children. Contingent upon the qualities of a child's symptoms, these medications might be useful sometimes however can accompany negative reactions and may build uneasiness in children with ADHD.

The instructive framework will be ease back to change so child rearing children with ADHD incorporates the employment of finding the most secure and most beneficial approaches to bolster their children and help them flourish in a framework that is not yet furnished to manage them as they seem to be.

Brainwave Training Can Provide Help for Children With ADHD

Much like a child can be instructed to ride a bicycle, a child can likewise be prepared to control the way they center attention. Through brainwave biofeedback preparing, likewise called electroencephalographic (EEG) biofeedback or neurofeedback, a child is given data to improve mind direction. This makes the essential modification which realize positive behavioral changes and self-control.

Figuring out how to adequately center attention with brainwave preparing exploits a child's capacity to effectively get to alpha cerebrum waves. Figuring out how to easily center attention in alpha is once in a while called "open concentration", and is the way to "superlearning" and improved critical thinking abilities. Instead of stifling a talented child with medications, even prevalent amusements like "PlayStation" and "Xbox" can be adjusted for successful brainwave preparing.

Other non-medicate related methodologies to help children with ADHD that function admirably with biofeedback are natural and homeopathic cures and eating routine conformities. Utilizing these in conjunction with mind preparing can be a compelling approach to quicken advance.

4 Ways To Help Children With ADHD Identify Facial Reactions

Children with ADHD regularly have problems comprehension individuals' facial responses. This is on account of they are perpetually circling doing several stuff while they infrequently have room schedule-wise to watch the emotional appearances on the characteristics of individuals around them. Along these lines, ADHD children never truly figure out how to comprehend the emotional demeanors on individuals' confronts, which means they can't tell whether somebody is upbeat, irate, disillusioned, miserable or humiliated. Subsequently, children with ADHD are regularly erroneously marked as 'narrow minded'.

Luckily, it is moderately simple to show children with ADHD to recognize outward appearances, which will in a roundabout way help to evacuate the "narrow minded" disgrace. Four of the best routes are:

Using kid's shows - Select a few significant toon characters and afterward request that the ADHD kid portray what these characters' emotions are. Keep in mind to bring up features, for example, the stature of the eyes, the inclination of the eye-temples and mouth, and wrinkles on the brow as markers in recognizing feelings.

Act it out - Teach the child by depicting the diverse parts of the face that contribute towards appearance. From that point onward, demonstrate these for the child with the goal that they know direct how the distinctive signals resemble. Afterward, get the child to demonstrate these expressions before a mirror. On the off chance that you happen to have a camcorder, then simply ahead and record these expressions for a better time and intelligent learning.

Using genuine pictures - Another action which is anything but difficult to actualize includes removing pictures of magazines or daily papers. Obviously the chose picture must portray an alternate outward appearance. Demonstrate these photos to the child and request that he figure and depict the facial responses.

Use the Internet - Cyberspace is brimming with clipart's and pictures of individuals doing a wide range of looks with their appearances. Download the fitting ones and afterward advise the ADHD child to recognize them.

Showing children with ADHD, or even ordinary children so far as that is concerned, to distinguish outward appearances or responses ought to be considered important in light of the fact that mislabeling individuals' looks and feelings whether at home, in school, or at social environment can make humiliation everybody concerned, including the children themselves. Accordingly, when children with ADHD seem egotistical or even demonstrate an absence of sympathy, denouncing fingers ought not be pointed at them promptly on the grounds that as a general rule they have not been instructed to distinguish facial responses or educated the fine purposes of compassion.

Yoga for Children With ADHD

Yoga for children with ADHD is a sensible arrangement. Yoga can be an unbelievably compelling apparatus in supporting children with ADHD to enhance their capacity to center and think well. There is a great deal of level headed discussion about the far reaching utilization of the mark ADHD among the restorative group. Be that as it may, the whole mess of diagnosing such a large number of children with ADHD is outside the domain of this article. Suffice it so say that perhaps a portion of the children marked with ADHD are carrying on rationally in a to some degree "wobbly" and separated world.

A genuine clinical conclusion of ADHD is frequently filled by a hereditary inclination, uneven neurochemistry and natural elements. Children who are battling with a great deal of uneasiness, despondency and ungrounded abundance vitality may likewise be determined to have ADHD. Other children might be genuinely enduring with an unevenness of neurotransmitters and may should be under the care of a doctor and additionally specialist. In any case, a normal routine of Yoga can ease the symptoms of ADHD and help a child to feel not so much overpowered but rather more ready to focus on the job needing to be done.

Now and again, ADHD might be exacerbated by a feeling of dejection, detachment and absence of attention that the child is encountering. The child may feel at a misfortune for a solid feeling of mooring from both his or her family and school. Rehearsing Yoga a few times each week with a similar gathering of understudies will help a child to security socially, advance a feeling of group connectedness and draw in the child in a balanced practice that supports both physical and psychological well-being.

Honing a fiery and fun arrangement of Yoga asanas a few times each week will likewise help a child to blaze off overabundance on edge vitality that might add to the absence of capacity to concentrate on one errand at any given moment. A consistent routine of Yoga likewise adjusts the sensory system and even adjust the endocrine framework, which may help a child to diminish the measure of prescription he or she is as of now taking. Do recall to please check with your child's specialist or therapist before changing the measurements of any professionally prescribed pharmaceutical.

The focusing and establishing practices of Yoga will likewise help a child to figure out how to center and think around one undertaking at any given moment. Simply honing Eagle Pose without falling over will be both fun and trying for a child with or without ADHD. As the child figures out how to trust him or herself in achieving the effective consummation of a progression of Yoga stances, the child will likewise figure out how to trust that he or she can finish thirty minutes of math or social reviews homework. In the majority of the previously mentioned ways, a normal routine of Yoga will bolster a child in being more grounded, less on edge, increment his or her level of self-regard, upgrade companionships and enhance the child's capacity to focus and concentrate on the job that needs to be done.

Chapter 25: Mastering Adhd In The Long Run

At the time of writing the latest research says that ADHD is a condition that you have to live with forever. At present there is no medicine that can cure ADHD. Therefore, it is important to accept your ADHD and the certain challenges that other people have not. It is important to discover what these challenges are. You have to make up your mind whether to live with the symptoms, or whether to make an effort to improve your lot. It is for example no need to make an effort to learn sit quietly in front of a computer if you have a job as a labourer or craftsman.

Symptoms of ADHD are also very different from person to person. The same applies to the severity of the symptoms. One can make a comparison with the strength of eyeglasses. Some need a prescription of +/- 10 and above, because they would be more or less blind without glasses. Others just use reading glasses with strength of

0.5. Just because you wear glasses, does not mean that you are blind. One can look at ADHD in the same way. Just because you have ADHD, it does not necessarily mean that you will not be able to function in society and the labour market. Therefore, it is important to identify what symptoms you are struggling with, and which difficulties you want to do something about.

Although the research says that ADHD is a permanent condition, there are actually certain things you can do. The brain can be trained as any other muscle in the body. Just as it is possible to train the brain to remember the first 500 decimal places in the number PI, it is also possible to train the brain to concentrate more. In the following paragraphs, I will touch on some topics that may help to improve concentration.

Avoid the "unhealthy carbohydrates"

Eat a healthy and balanced diet without too many easily digestible carbohydrates. There is not yet any clear evidence that a healthy diet has a positive effect on ADHD. That said, I am in no doubt that I can feel the difference whether I have been eating healthily or not. To understand the context, I will briefly quote an article from the Danish magazine "Illustrated science" about how digestion works in relation to sugar:

[1]This is how you digest

Food is broken down by enzymes in the digestive system, into glucose among other things. It will be absorbed through the small intestine and get into the blood.

The sugar is carried around with the blood and inhibits some nerve cells in the brain that produces a special alertness hormone, orexin. This means that we get tired.

Finally, the sugar reaches the muscle, liver and fatty tissues by way of insulin from the pancreas.

When you have ADHD, you already use large amounts of energy. You do not have the same filters, to screen out sensory impressions that other people have. If you eat a lot of starch or simple carbohydrates, the blood sugar quickly rises. The blood has a high content of sugar over a long period as the production of insulin has only just started. This means that the orexin-producing nerve cells are also inhibited over a long period; with the result we are tiring quickly. The reduced level of the hormone orexin is therefore inhibiting your ability to concentrate.

Conclusion

While we have included lots of information inside we know we have merely scratched the surface of all there is to know about ADHD. Inside you've learned how to identify if ADHD is the problem with your child, what signs to look for, and how to know if you need to seek a diagnosis or not.

You've also learned how your relationship with your child can have a direct impact on his success. Positive interactions build up self-esteem in a child that is already struggling to fit in, and negative responses can be like a landmine poised to blow at any moment.

You've learned how to identify your child executive skills and determine which ones are weakest and then what to do about them.

We've given you some practical suggestions on ways to teach your child both informally and formally and the signs along with ways to measure their progress.

A step-by-step approach to teaching them to how to utilize the skills they have to accomplish just about any task.

No question, we included a lot of information in this book, and likely your head is probably spinning right now. Still, take your time and let your own mind absorb what's here and put it into practice. That way everyone will benefit from these guidelines and thus reap the reward in the process.

www.ingramcontent.com/pod-product-compliance
Lightning Source LLC
Chambersburg PA
CBHW051721020426
42333CB00014B/1086